The Graduate Course You Never Had

How to Develop, Manage, and Market a Flourishing Private Mental Health Practice—With and Without Managed Care

LARRY F. WALDMAN, Ph.D., ABPP

DEDICATION

For all my fellow professional service providers who strive to be as professional in running their business as they are in helping their patients/clients achieve a better quality of life.

ACKNOWLEDGMENTS

I especially thank my wife, Nan, for her support and encouragement, in good and tough times, through our nearly four decades of marriage. She is the best "partner" I could ever have.

I also am grateful for Larry Zeger, LCSW; Karl Riem, Ed.D.; Larry Beer, Esq.; June Fabiano; Jon Ward; and Andy Renk; for their content recommendations and constructive editorial comments.

And for the many hundreds of patients/clients I've counseled during thirty-plus years of practice. There have been times when I have learned more from them than they have from me.

Author's Note

It is said that if you want to be a millionaire you can accelerate the process by associating with millionaires, getting inside their heads, and learning how to think the way they do.

Although this book is not about becoming a millionaire, I think the same learning process can be applied to becoming the best mental health care provider you can be—and do so by running your practice following a proven business model.

You might have heard the old adage that a "bird in the hand is worth two birds in the bush."

Well, in this course that you never had in school, consider me your "bird in the hand." This is your opportunity to get inside my head, learn how I think, and learn how to develop and maintain a quality, profitable practice just as I have done.

I'm in the twilight of a career that has spanned over 30 years of mental health care practice that—yes—I run effectively using proven business principles that really do work for those who are willing to apply them.

No matter what stage you are in as a mental health care provider – still in school, just out of school, being client-fed by a Managed Care company, or have an independent practice with primarily cash-pay clientele – you will find nuggets on these pages that will help you build, increase, and maintain a more profitable business.

Dig in. Learn. Apply.

Larry Waldman

UCS PRESS PMB 119
1702 W. Camelback Rd. # 13
Phoenix, AZ 85015

UCS PRESS is an imprint of MarJim Books, Inc.

Cover design by Andy Renk

First edition, first printing, March 2010

Printed in the United States of America

ISBN: 978-0-943247-97-7

TABLE OF CONTENTS

To laugh is to risk appearing a fool,
To weep is to risk appearing sentimental
To reach out to another is to risk involvement,
To expose feelings is to risk exposing your true self
To place your ideas and dreams before a crowd is to risk their loss
To love is to risk not being loved in return,
To hope is to risk despair,
To try is to risk to failure.
But risks must be taken because the greatest hazard in life is to risk nothing.
The person who risks nothing, does nothing, has nothing, is nothing.
He may avoid suffering and sorrow,
But he cannot learn, feel, change, grow or live.
Chained by his servitude he is a slave who has forfeited all freedom.
Only a person who risks is free.

Anon

(*seen variously attributed with slight variations to William Arthur Ward, Ralph Waldo Emerson, Leo Buscaglia, and anonymous*)

CHAPTER ONE

MY STORY

I knew very early on in my training that I wanted to develop and run a private psychological practice. Nevertheless, I never had the opportunity to take a course or as much as a seminar on the basics of developing, running and growing a private mental health practice. In the 1970's there was little literature available on the subject. For that matter, not much has changed in the ensuing three decades.

Initially, I began working in the field of psychology as a school psychologist. After I obtained my Ph.D. I continued to work for the school for a time but also did evaluations on the side for another psychologist in private practice located on the opposite end of town. This psychologist, more or less, began to mentor me in the business of private practice.

Since my "mentor" was planning to retire around the time I intended to leave my school psychology job and go into private practice, it was agreed that I would buy his practice. Thus, in January 1980 I went into private practice. My mentor stayed several months afterward to ease the transition.

I was glad I "bought" the practice (it was not much money because I had little at the time) because I instantly had an office, furniture, file cabinets, test kits and forms, a phone system, and a trained receptionist/secretary/biller. The only thing I did not have, of course, were clients/patients.

Because there were two other suites in the office, I took on two other psychologists—who happened to be husband and wife—and had just come to Phoenix. We had a hand-shake agreement on an arrangement where I supplied everything and received a percent of their receivables.

For the first six months or so, I spent more time out of the office than in it, as I very actively marketed our "group." I also rented some office space and services to a psychiatrist—who sent us referrals.

For the first year I barely earned enough to cover expenses. My family and I lived off savings and the State retirement reimbursement I took when I left the School District as a school psychologist.

By year two I was beginning to make some money. I continued to add some part-time people, like a tutor, speech and language therapist, and a counselor.

By year three the office was coming along, and I was making two to three times more than I did as a school psychologist. I was enjoying the fruits of my labor and I was about to ask the two psychologists to become full-partners in the practice for a small fee, since I had done all the work putting the practice together. We agreed to discuss terms after I got back from my first vacation in three years—in the summer of 1983.

When I returned from vacation I learned that my prospective partners, instead of aligning with me, had decided to set up in another office in the same complex—and the secretary and counselor were going with them, as well. What I realized then was that my prospective partners initially were accepting of our business relationship when there was little income and I was paying the bills. However, when the practice began to make money they became resentful of the income I was making from their labor—forgetting about my initial investment. Hence, I inadvertently fostered a classic "hostile-dependent" relationship.

Since my lease on the suite was nearly up, and I did not feel like starting completely over, I closed my practice and joined the largest private mental health group in Phoenix at the time, which was based in a hospital with several different psychiatric programs. The group consisted of four psychiatrists, one nurse practitioner, eight psychologists, and two or three therapists. The practice essentially owned the various psychiatric units, and very quickly I was extremely busy doing inpatient as well as outpatient work. Twelve-hour days, six days per week, was the norm.

After about six months of working 60-70 hours per week, my wife began to complain that if I was going to be gone working so much, where was all the money? My response was that I had to build up accounts receivable and then the money would begin to flow. Unfortunately, by the end of the first year or so, I was earning about half as much as I had earned in my own little practice before—but was working twice as much.

After a few more months the financial situation for me was still no better. A client I was seeing for several months happened to note to me that he was wondering when I was going to bill him and his insurance company, since he had received no paperwork of any sort related to his treatment with me. With that information I left a message with the office manager asking why this client and his insurance had not been billed. When I did not get an answer after a few days, I met with her and demanded an answer. I requested that she explain, in detail, how the billing procedure worked.

What very quickly became apparent is that the office manager had no idea how the billing process, from the beginning to the end, actually worked. Moreover, when I met with the back office staff, they, too, were quite unclear about the entire process.

I reviewed the problem at the next partners' meeting but, surprisingly, the partners' response was essentially to leave the situation alone. To make my point I proceeded to train one of the more enthusiastic back office staff persons in the process of insurance verification, billing, and re-contacting. In three months my accounts receivable was the highest in the group; I was earning more than psychiatrists who were billing more than $350,000.00 per year—and had been doing so for years! Again, amazingly, the partners' reaction was that I was "meddling where I didn't belong."

I left that large group in 1983 and took my accounts receivable with me. I set up another practice with another therapist from the group who was also frustrated by the lack of income despite working very hard. We hired a secretary who worked for the two of us—whom I trained. Within three months she collected 90 percent of the old accounts receivable from the group practice for both of us.

I thrived in my simple practice doing inpatient and outpatient work and consulting. I made the most money ever in my career in the late 80's to early 90's—better than a quarter of a million dollars per year.

As Managed Care began to get stronger in Phoenix, I began to think about again becoming a member of a group; reducing overhead increasingly seemed to be a good idea. Thus, in 1995 I joined a group practice, which included psychiatrists, psychologists, and therapists. The group was essentially a collection of individuals practicing separately—which is exactly what I was looking for.

In 2004, with three partners—a psychologist and two psychiatrists—we bought and built our own office. We designed it specifically for our needs, with particular attention paid to soundproofing. We four partners rent the spare suites to other mental health practitioners. The rental income essentially pays our costs and expenses.

I remain quite successful, with a diverse, largely cash-pay practice, even in a difficult economy. By owning our office, I have major tax advantages, and the building has appreciated significantly in value.

What did all this experience teach me about mental health practice?

1. Get all contractual agreements in writing.

2. Do not form hostile-dependent financial arrangements with employees/colleagues.

3. Learn and understand the <u>business</u> of mental health practice well.

4. Learn the process of insurance billing well.

5. Train, treat, and pay your staff well.

6. Specialize and diversify.

7. Become creative in thinking of ways you earn income and find clients—especially those bearing cash.

My practice today is multifaceted and involves the following:

Cognitive-behavioral and/or solution-focused therapy with children, adolescents, and adults.

Parenting training.

Marital training.

Psycho-educational evaluations.

Psycho-educational evaluations for school districts.

Psychological evaluations.

Psychological evaluations for the Court.

Custody evaluations.

Parenting Coordinating.

Consultations to personal injury, defense, estate planning, and immigration attorneys.

Consulting to Social Security.

Selling my books and CDs.

Professional speaking.

Important points to remember in CHAPTER ONE:

1. Get all agreements in writing.

2. Do not form hostile-dependent financial relationships with colleagues.

3. Learn to consider your practice as a business and treat it as such.

4. Learn the insurance game.

5. Train, treat, and pay staff well—it pays.

6. Specialize—and diversify.

7. Become creative in how to earn income in mental health other than sitting in a room with a client.

Action steps to take from CHAPTER ONE:

1. Have an attorney review your lease, rental agreements with tenants, financial arrangements with colleagues, employment contract(s), and other pertinent legal documents.

2. Consider revising your financial arrangement with colleagues to get out from under a hostile-dependent relationship.

3. Consider giving your staff a raise accompanied by more responsibility to increase loyalty.

4. Read a book and schedule a workshop to begin to develop a new "specialty."

Man who stand on hill with mouth open will wait long time for roast duck to drop in.

Confucius

Don't wait until everything is just right. It will never be perfect. There will always be challenges, obstacles and less than perfect conditions. So what. Get started now. With each step you take, you will grow stronger and stronger, more and more skilled, more and more self-confident and more and more successful.

Mark Victor Hansen

CHAPTER TWO

PRIVATE PRACTICE AS A BUSINESS

Introduction

We have all heard the generalization that physicians are considered to be poor business persons. Well, mental health practitioners are far, far worse. Mental health professionals are individuals who want to help other people. They are not in the mental health field for the money, typically. Most mental health practitioners have never taken a basic course in business and many do not consider their "practice" to be a true business.

The basic truth, of course, is that every mental health practice is a business—albeit a small one, whether the practitioner wants to think of it as such, or not. As a mental health business, the professional provides a service—typically psychotherapy—and hopefully the professional receives a fee for that service. From the fees the practitioner receives expenses must be paid—rent, secretarial services, phone, supplies, license fees, insurance, test kits, furniture, computers, continuing education, taxes, and unexpected needs that might arise. What is left after all these expenses are covered is profit—which the mental health professional needs to survive.

Regardless of how dearly the mental health professional wants to help people, unless there are sufficient and steady profits in the practice, the professional will not be able to afford to remain in practice for very long. Therefore, a private mental health practice is a business, and for it to be successful, it should be considered and conducted as one.

When I was in graduate school my fellow students and I often talked about how we were going to become wealthy soon by way of having a large practice in which many clients would pay us huge fees. That was our fantasy. It certainly was not a reality.

On occasion I will speak to graduate students regarding private practice. I am always impressed with how unrealistic these students are. The reality is that few if any graduates of a mental health program receive any training in the business of mental health. Moreover, we often receive no training whatsoever in how to develop, grow, manage, and, especially, market a mental health practice. With one exception, health care providers of all types receive no training in the business component of their chosen field. The only health care provider group of which I am aware where their training includes practice-building, marketing and management are chiropractors.

This concept reminds me of the "baby course" my wife and I had to take years ago before our first son was born, so I could be in attendance in the delivery room. For eight consecutive Wednesday evenings, we went to the hospital and listened to a nurse speak about embryology, the birth process, and a bit about basic care and feeding of the neonate.

At the end of the series I asked the nurse in charge if there was ever any thought given to devoting time to speaking about basic child development and child discipline concepts. I concluded my point to the nurse by saying, "You have taught us well how to have our baby, but what are we supposed to do with it once we bring it home?" By the same token, graduate schools teach us how to provide psychotherapy but teach us nothing about how to operate the business of providing those mental health services.

Private mental health practice as a business model

Suppose you wanted to design the perfect business. What would be some of the basic elements of that business?

> The product or service of the business would have wide appeal.

> The product or service could be provided easily.

The product or service could be provided cheaply.

Payment for the product or service would be quick, simple and easy.

The product or service could be available 24/7.

The product or service could be provided cheaply by other than the business owner.

The product or service would lend itself to frequent repeat business.

The business could be duplicated.

The list above, I submit, comprises some of the basic components of an ideal business. Along these lines, it seems to me that owning a McDonald's franchise, for example, closely approximates the ideal business: McDonald's has a wide appeal, especially to children, but also to many adults, as well. McDonald's are everywhere; they are easy to find; and it is simple and quick to place your order and receive your food. How the food is prepared is automated and regulated and is easily and quickly done. Payment for the product is quick, simple, and easy—and usually in cash.

McDonald's are open from early morning to late at night, nearly every day of the year.

McDonald's are usually staffed by adolescents earning minimum wage, supervised by a manager—not the owner. The staff are not paid that well. Customers who patronize McDonald's usually do so several times per month. A McDonald's restaurant franchise can make an owner rich, with the owner rarely, if ever, being there. If the owner chooses, he or she can buy more than one franchise and become even wealthier.

Given the basic elements of an ideal business, such as a McDonald's franchise, consider the business model for a private mental health practice:

While mental health professionals believe everybody could benefit from psychotherapy, most laypersons do not agree with this notion and, in fact, have an aversion to the concept of mental health treatment. We all understand there is a stigma attached to mental health treatment. Even individuals who seek mental health treatment often have some trepidation about it and certainly want to keep the process confidential—which, of course, is most appropriate and their right. Even if we were to provide our service for free, a large number of persons would not take the offer. For many persons, we cannot even give our services away! Thus, the service we provide does not pass the test of "wide appeal."

Any mental health professional will vouch for the fact that offering psychotherapy is rewarding but also stressful and challenging. Also, unlike other health care providers, including psychiatrists, where other professionals can substitute for the primary caregiver, in the field of psychotherapy only the original therapist can provide the service. Again, the business of mental health fails the test of providing the service easily and cheaply—and also fails with respect to the business being duplicated, as the therapist cannot hire a manager or another therapist to provide the service for the same patient.

Therapists typically see their clients from as early as eight or nine in the morning to as late as eight or nine in the evening and do not usually work weekends or holidays. Therapists usually see no more than six clients—customers—per day. There are only so many hours a week that a therapist might reasonably see a client. Thus, again, mental health fails with respect to being open for business 24/7/365.

I make it a point when I terminate with a client to leave the door open for them to return at a later date. Many therapists do not do this and, as a result, get few clients who return for additional treatment. Many clients thank me for my service but say they hope they will not need to return. Once again, mental health practice fails with respect to frequent repeat business.

Finally, when insurance is involved, the payment process is anything but simple and easy. Most people have no idea what their medical insurance covers or how it works. With respect to mental health coverage, the typical person knows even less. Most clients have no idea what a deductible or co-pay is. Many clients believe they can see a mental health professional, offer their insurance card, assuming they brought it with them, and the mental health professional will simply handle everything else. Again, mental health practice fails with respect to the ease and simplicity of payment for the service.

The bottom line in the practice of mental health is that the mental health professional only earns income when he/she and the client/patient are in the same room at the same time—and the insurance, if you are using it, is valid. As a business model, then, the private practice of mental health, frankly, stinks! Therefore, the mental health professional must take advantage of every available hour to maximize his or her earning potential.

Valuing your time and service

Recently, I was at a conference and during the break I was having a conversation with a colleague. We were talking about cash-pay practice, and he jokingly said, "I wouldn't pay $125 an hour to see myself." A basic tenet of business is that you must have complete faith in your product or service to be able to successfully promote it. If my colleague does not value his service at $125 a session, he should lower his fee to the point where he does value it—or consider changing careers. I certainly can understand why he is having difficulty developing a fee-for-service practice when he, in fact, does not believe his service is worth the fee he is charging.

We have all heard the old saying "You get what you pay for." How much value does the man or the woman on the street assign to psychotherapy (our service/product) when all they have to pay for it is a 10 or 20 dollar co-pay? We mental health providers are such bleeding hearts and so much want to help people, that we regularly discount our fees or drop them all together. I submit we are not helping our clients by doing so, but, instead, are simply reducing the perceived value of our service. Moreover, with Managed Care making our service appear so cheap, the system further devalues our service.

Recently, a patient of mine asked that I write a report of her treatment and send it to her attorney. I told her I would be glad to do so but there would be a charge for that service. (Many of my colleagues would do this for free.) The client responded by saying that she thought I was supposed to be keeping notes of our sessions. I said I did have treatment notes, of course, but they were not in a report format. If she wanted a report, I would have to review the 10 treatment sessions we had, compose and dictate a letter, and pay my transcriptionist to type it. That process would take about an hour and a half, and, with the transcription fee, would cost $200—and insurance does not pay for that procedure.

The client decided to first check with her attorney but after doing so called back and said to go ahead and write the report. I learned later that her attorney was charging her $350 per hour. (It probably cost her $50 just to check with him or her to learn what I told her previously that my notes were not in the preferred format.) The point, of course, was whose time did this client value more—the attorney charging $350 per hour or the psychologist getting a $20 co-pay? Again, we mental health professionals have done a poor job of getting the general population to truly value our service.

Suppose your child or significant other was having ongoing migraine headaches and you desired to seek help for them. What would you do? You would likely speak to your family physician or pediatrician and get the name of a good neurologist. You might also call other persons you know who might also know of a neurologist. Once you decided on a physician you would call that office and schedule an appointment. At the appointed time you would come with your child or significant other and hopefully receive the appropriate treatment.

I do not believe you would do the following:

Call five or six neurologists out of the phone book and ask to speak to each doctor individually, so you could discuss the case with all of them. (The physicians' staffs, in most cases, would not even let that happen.) Schedule appointments with all five doctors but keep only one of them and never cancel the other four.

Most people would never conceive of doing the above in the effort to secure treatment with a neurologist, for example, but many people behave exactly in this manner when attempting to make an appointment with a mental health provider—and we clinicians continue to allow it!

When individuals ask to speak to me directly before they make their first appointment, I always immediately ask them who referred them. If they cannot give me a positive answer, I then ask who else they have contacted. If they note several other providers, I tell them that one of them previously mentioned would likely serve their needs well, thank them for calling, and hang up. In my 30-plus years of practice I have learned well that these calls can take better than 30 minutes of my time, rarely result in an appointment, and even if an appointment is made, the odds are good that the client will not show. The reason I say this is because this person took the time of five mental health providers and thus is clearly displaying they have little or no respect for these professionals' time—and I do not wish to see such a client. If you allow yourself to get involved in a clinical discussion with this "shopper" (as I like to term these callers) you may well be extending yourself with respect to liability.

At times, I get calls from prospective clients who request that I spend considerable time on the phone with them before we meet, "to see if we are a good fit." Do we do this with physicians, attorneys, dentists, or accountants? No. I tell such clients that much of what the first session is for is for me to get a relevant history and for us to see if there is a "fit." It is as if someone walked into a grocery store, took two pieces of bread out of a loaf on the shelf, opened a jar of peanut butter and a jar of jam, and had themselves a PB&J to see if they liked that store's products. No other professionals allow clients to have a free "try out," so why do we mental health professionals continue to allow it? We must do a much better job of encouraging the public to value our service.

If clients no-show or late-cancel their first appointment with me, they are told that they are required to first pay the full, cash fee (whether they have insurance or not) for the missed appointment before they can schedule another one with me. In truth, only 10 to 20 percent of people do pay for the no-show or late-cancellation, but, nevertheless, I am teaching them that my time is valuable. Perhaps they will treat the next mental health professional they see with more consideration. If they pay for the missed appointment, I probably will want them as a patient because they are showing they value my time. My experience is that most mental health providers will allow the client who no-showed to reschedule, without any penalty, because we "care," and sometimes we need the clients, but frequently we are simply "stood up" again. We all know what happens when inappropriate behavior is reinforced.

In general, if a client is taking your time and not paying for it, they are disrespecting and not valuing your professional service and we mental health providers should stop allowing it. Our business is our time. When someone takes it without payment, they are essentially stealing from you. I value my training, experience, time, and the service I provide, and I expect my clients/patients to do the same.

Make a plan

As in running any business, a mental health professional should use the services of an accountant or bookkeeper to manage the financial books, and keep track of expenses and profits. A medical biller, either in-house or as a consultant, may be needed, especially if you run a practice that is comprised largely of managed care clients. An attorney will also prove useful to review leases, rental contracts, and employment contracts, and other situations where a legal opinion is helpful.

Finally, you do not begin building a house without a set of blueprints, so you should not begin a practice without a business plan. In a business plan you outline the specific goals and objectives to beginning, developing, and maintaining a private mental health practice. A basic plan should outline financial goals, basic expenses, a marketing plan, and a timetable by which to accomplish the stated objectives.

Is private practice right for you?

I have talked about many of the advantages of private practice—autonomy, and the opportunity to make more money. Before we go much farther, though, I should note that there are several issues that you need to consider before deciding to make a career in private practice:

> **1.** Bc organized. If you work for a school district, agency, prison, or hospital, for example, you just show up and assume the office will be clean, the support staff will be available, and the phones, lights, and photocopy machine will all be in order. In a private practice all these areas—and many more—are your responsibility. In a private practice which, remember, is a business, you will be responsible for many things beyond seeing your clients. I have known several mental health professionals who were excellent clinicians but were too disorganized to successfully run their business of private practice.
>
> **2.** Be independent. A little known fact of private practice is that social and professional isolation can be a problem. If you are busy, which of course is

your objective, you will be spending most of your days in your office sitting across from your clients. There will be relatively little time to schmooze with colleagues. While you will need to obtain your CEs, in private practice you are less inclined to take large amounts of time out of the office because that represents lost income—which is not an issue for clinicians working in the public sector.

3. Be flexible. Clients will not show up, not pay their bill, and disappoint you. You will also have to learn to live with a paycheck that varies from week to week and month to month. Over the years many professionals have told me they shied away from private practice because they could not deal with not knowing how much they were going to earn every month.

4. Be entrepreneurial. To be successful in private practice you must be business-minded and innovative. By and large, Managed Care notwithstanding, you must secure your clients—they do not come to you. Finding enough clients to see is certainly not an issue when you work in the public sector. I know of many mental health providers, and also several attorneys, who simply were not interested in "hustling" for clients.

5. Be prepared to work hard. To be successful in private practice means you will work more than 40 hours per week, you rarely will be home for dinner by 6 pm, and you will take work home. You will have to learn to pace yourself and develop the ability to be sharp for eight to 10 clients on many days.

Important points to remember in CHAPTER TWO:

1. The private practice of mental health, from a business model perspective, is poor. Therefore, the practitioner must take full advantage of every available hour.

2. We have to value our time and service, if we expect our clients to.

3. Use the services of an accountant and an attorney to help run your business.

4. Develop a business plan.

5. Ask yourself if you are cut out for private practice.

Action steps to take from CHAPTER TWO:

1. Consult an accountant to review your business plan and analyze the financial status of your practice. (You will need him or her to do your taxes, anyway.)

2. Speak with your staff about the concept of the practice as a business and discuss ways to increase revenue and reduce costs. (Often, saving a dollar is easier than earning one—and you don't have to pay taxes on the money you save.)

What these people in the sports world said about taking action:

What keeps me going is goals.

Muhammad Ali

If you keep thinking about what you want to do or what you hope will happen, you don't do it, and it won't happen.

Joe Dimaggio

The secret to success is to start from scratch and keep on scratching.

Dennis Green

You have to make it happen.

Joe Greene

When all is said and done, more is said than done.

Lou Holtz

CHAPTER THREE

GETTING STARTED

Part or Full-Time?

Some individuals are willing and able to jump into private practice on a full-time basis, but many are unable to do so. To leave a full-time job with an agency or school district, for example, to dive into a full-time practice can be frightening and financially intimidating. I recommend that if you are contemplating going full-time into private practice, you should have saved enough funds to pay for basic professional and personal expenses for a minimum of six months, preferably for a year. The number one reason businesses fail—and remember your private practice is a small business—is under-capitalization. Many would-be private practitioners have to give up their dreams of private practice because they run out of funds before their private practice is sufficiently developed to sustain them financially. In these cases the practitioners have to close their start-up practice and return to working for someone else.

I believe there are few things more rewarding than starting and running your own successful business. Being able to call your own shots, set your own policies, and determine your own hours, is quite satisfying. Moreover, when you are working for yourself you are more motivated to perform at your best.

I have been going to the gym four times per week in the morning for decades. Exercising, as all mental health professionals know well, is very healthy for the body and the mind. Only by working for myself over the past 30 years could I find the time to regularly do my workouts and maintain a high level of health and fitness.

For some practitioners, moving into private practice on a part-time basis is more feasible and less financially threatening.

There are several options to consider:

To begin with, if you are already working full-time with an agency, the State, or with a school district, your days are full but your evenings and weekends are likely open. You could begin seeing patients as soon as possible after work on a weekday evening, and be able to see two, three, or even four clients at night. You could also see clients on Saturday. Therefore, if you really wanted to hustle, you could potentially see nearly 20 clients per week in your part-time practice. Clearly, this schedule of working full-time and seeing 15 to 20 clients in the evenings and on Saturday would be exhausting and probably not something you would want to do for a long time. The goal of this set-up would be to save enough money to launch a full-time practice after a few months.

For some practitioners, maintaining a small, part-time practice, in addition to a full-time job, is a safe, acceptable arrangement—though tiring. It has been my experience, though, that if you truly want a full-time private practice, by maintaining a full-time job and seeing private patients on a part-time basis, you will likely neither have the time nor the energy to adequately market your practice to develop it into a full-time one.

Office/Practice arrangements

There are a number of different practice arrangements you might want to consider:

1. You could join a group practice in which all the providers bill under the same tax ID number. Usually you will be compensated by way of a set salary or by a percent of billings for receivables. (In my experience, approximately 50% of billings or about 65% of receivables is common.)

The advantage of this system is that you have colleagues to consult with and everything is already in place—furniture, phone system, secretary, and billing system. The disadvantage is that you have little control.

2. You could join a group practice in which each provider bills under his or her separate tax ID. In this situation you usually pay your share of expenses. The primary advantage of this system is that you not only have all the advantages of a group practice and have basic control over your particular practice; you also are able to share the costs. The primary disadvantage is that you are essentially completely responsible for finding your own clients/patients.

3. You could rent office space in a physician's office. Today, many physicians have extra space and would be more than happy to lease out some of it. This arrangement would likely provide for reception, a phone system, and furniture. Very importantly, this situation could and should also supply referrals. Therefore, it is important to choose your physician group wisely. Obviously, if you want to work with children and parents, check out a pediatrician's office; an OBG office, for example, would supply referrals of women, marital issues, and sexual issues. A GP's office would generally provide all sorts of referrals. Of course, a psychiatrist's office would be an excellent place in which a psychologist or therapist could practice.

The basic disadvantage of such an arrangement is that you would have to do your own scheduling, phone calling, and billing. Moreover, it should be understood that if you align yourself with a particular physician's office, it is unlikely you will receive referrals from any other doctors. Therefore, if you opt for this arrangement, be certain that your physicians can supply a sufficient number of referrals to keep you as busy as you wish to be.

4. How long do you intend to be in practice—10, 20, 25, 30 years? Most individuals, in the future, are probably not going to be able to retire until they reach their late 60's at least. (As of this writing, the age for full Social Security benefits is 66.) Therefore, if you complete graduate school around age 30, you will likely have a private practice career of 30 to 35 years—or more.

If you pay office rent for these 30-plus years, with the average monthly rent over that period of time being approximately $1,000, you will have paid about one-third of a million dollars in rent over your career. If you paid a third of million dollars for an office over 30 years, I would assume you would prefer to own it—not make your landlord rich. Therefore, I believe the best office arrangement is one in which you own your own office space.

Optimally, I recommend that you save, beg, borrow, or steal (not really) a down payment and purchase a condo office, a home office properly zoned, or a small office building in an area in which you believe you want to practice for some time. You can then design and retrofit the property to your needs, including the necessary soundproofing. If you cannot afford to buy the property on your own, you can form an LLC with one or more other mental health providers and do the deal together. (Be sure to use an attorney for that partnership agreement.)

In addition to a waiting room and secretarial area the office should have several extra suites that you (and your partners) can lease out. Moreover, you should train your office person in handling the phone, reception, scheduling, collecting through the window, and billing. Depending on the number of providers and how busy they become, you may need an additional part-time biller or consulting biller.

In this arrangement you will be able to lease out the suites at a $1,000 to $1,500 per month (at today's rates) for a full-service office—furniture, phone, copy machine, fax, reception, phone handling, scheduling, basic secretarial services, and billing.

An office of 1,500 to 2,000 square feet should provide at least six nice suites. Thus, if you own the office and received rent from five suites, you would have a potential monthly income of about $7,500, which should more than cover your monthly office expenses. With this arrangement your cost of overhead for your practice is then about zero, you have not created a hostile-dependent financial relationship with your tenants/colleagues, you get all the tax breaks, and you earn the appreciation on the building.

If things go as planned, when I retire and sell my share of our building, I hope to glean a quarter of a million dollars in appreciation. Wouldn't it be nice to earn income not only from providing mental health services but also from appreciating real estate?

It is important that you choose your tenants carefully. Your tenants/colleagues should each have liability insurance and practice in a thoughtful, effective, and most ethical manner. Although you and each of your tenants/colleagues are in independent practice, if one member of the "group" is censured or sued for improper conduct, it reflects poorly on the entire group.

Additionally, when screening tenants, you want practitioners that have complementary practices. If all the providers in the office are, say, interested working primarily with children, you would all be competing for the same clients and there would be few cross-referrals. Instead, try to find tenants with various practice specialties—such as child, adult, family, forensic, biofeedback, EMDR, or chemical dependency. With a mixed group of tenants they will not compete for the same clients, tenants can market themselves and the "group," and there is good likelihood there will be cross-referrals within the office.

I am the only member in our office that conducts formal psychological testing and evaluations. Thus, I receive numerous referrals for evaluations from my colleagues every year. I especially like doing evaluations because they are "big ticket" (large fee) procedures and most often involve cash-pay.

By designing a practice in this manner there is no hostile-dependent relationship. In fact, the relationships are collegial and supportive.

I believe an office arrangement such as this has all the benefits of a group practice but none of the disadvantages. If you design your office in this manner it is important to have a clause in each registration form noting that each provider in the office is an independent practitioner—and have the clients initial that section on the registration form.

Secretarial options

It is probably apparent by now that I believe in having a full-time secretary. The first contact a patient or prospective client has with you is likely to be with the secretary. That first contact should be a prompt and positive one with a secretary/receptionist who is professional, courteous, caring, knowledgeable, and loyal to you and the practice.

It has been my experience that a sharp, well-trained secretary can completely service four to five busy therapists, exclusive of billing and extensive report typing. Psychiatrists require more intense secretarial/back office assistance. The billing and report typing, I believe, should be handled separately because this work cannot be done at the same time the secretary is greeting clients, scheduling them, taking money, answering the phone, and verifying insurance. I recommend, therefore, the billing and extensive transcription be handled separately by either an outside billing or transcription service or a part-time person you train who can do it at the office or even in his or her home.

As any mental professional knows, an individual does not suddenly decide to receive mental health treatment and immediately make a phone call to a nearby mental health provider. Instead, most individuals contemplate seeking mental health treatment for some time before they finally act on that idea. They usually get a provider name or two, or three, or even four, from their insurance company or possibly from a friend or colleague, their primary care physician, a pediatrician, their attorney, someone from their child's school, an information and referral service, or the Internet. If they are with Managed Care they pick their therapist out of a book or go to the one directed by intake. When they finally make that call, regardless of how they got your name, they want to speak to a live person and schedule an appointment. They truly do not want to hear a recording and have to leave a message and wait for a return call—and possibly play phone tag. The odds are high that if they call the first provider on their list and get a recording, they will proceed to call the second, or the third, until they get a live person to talk to. Think of all the effort you expended to get that client to call. What a shame to finally get that call but you were not there to receive it.

On more occasions than I can count, when I ask the client at the beginning of the first session, "How did you find me?" The answer I often receive is, "You were the first office I could talk to." Thus, having a good secretary who answers the phone quickly and appropriately will likely bring you a number of clients that you would not otherwise have received. Besides, if the secretary's salary is being spread over several providers, the cost of the service is truly nominal—yet is so valuable.

There are days I see 10 patients—Mondays and Thursdays. At the end of such a long day I do not have the inclination or the energy to file charts, call back clients with general questions, verify insurance, or do the billing. If I had to do all this work, I would be unable to see as many clients—maybe only five or six. The point, of course, is that my secretary has made me thousands of dollars over the years.

I recognize, of course, that if you are just starting out in practice and you do not have a patient to your name, you are not going to hire a full-time secretary. Initially, you could do all the work the secretary would do because you have the time. As you get more clients, though, you could use a remote answering service. If you are the owner or member of a group practice, though, you will want to hire and train a secretary very early on.

Important points to remember in CHAPTER THREE:

1. You can go into private practice on a full- or part-time basis.
2. Have sufficient capital saved to sustain yourself and your practice when you go into practice.
3. Working a full-time job and carrying a part-time practice is fine, but it will likely be too demanding to develop a full-time practice.
4. There are various office/practice arrangements to consider. Owning your office is best.
5. Having a well-trained, loyal secretary pays dividends.

Action steps to take from CHAPTER THREE:

1. If you ultimately desire a full-time practice but are starting out on a part-time basis, set a ("drop dead") date by which you will "take the leap" to go into it on a full-time basis.

2. Review your savings and ensure you have enough money to fund your practice and live for six months to a year—most especially if you are taking the full-time "leap."

3. Give real thought to owning your office. Look at properties in the area you desire. If necessary, speak with fellow mental health professionals regarding forming a partnership to purchase some space.

It is not good enough for things to be planned -- they still have to be done; for the intention to become a reality, energy has to be launched into operation.

Pir Vilayat Khan

The sure conviction that we could if we wanted to is the reason so many good minds are idle.

G. C. (Georg Christoph) Lichtenberg

Often the difference between a successful person and a failure is not one has better abilities or ideas, but the courage that one has to bet on one's ideas, to take a calculated risk – and to act.

Maxwell Maltz

CHAPTER FOUR

PRACTICE MANAGEMENT CONCEPTS

Correct Forms

You first want to have an appropriate registration form. It should have space for all the information necessary for insurance billing and collecting. It should also have the required information to be HIPPA compliant. I suggest you contact your state organization to get information on what is necessary and appropriate.

The form should also clearly delineate your policies concerning billing, late cancellations, and no-shows, and any other pertinent information. There should be a place where the client initials that they have read and understood each provision. (As noted previously, if you have a group practice of independent providers, there should also be a clause that denotes that each professional is practicing independently—and the client should initial that clause as well.)

Special informed consents

If you are doing something outside the realm of traditional psychotherapy, such as custody evaluations, you will want to have the client receive and sign a separate informed consent specific to that procedure. Accordingly, when I do a custody evaluation or parenting coordinating, I have each adult participant sign a specific informed consent. A major reason mental health professionals get in trouble with their respective boards is that their clients were unaware that something negative could happen (such as not get their way with respect to a child visitation issue) or what the cost of some service would be. Too often, the professional has no document to prove that they went over those issues with the client. My informed consents are very specific, are signed and dated by the client, and the client is given a copy of what they signed.

Get their e-mail

If it is not already on your registration form you should immediately revise your form so that there is a place for the client's e-mail address. I only wish I had done this many years ago. Had I done so, I would now have an e-mail list of past clients and referral sources that probably would number several hundred or more.

I believe this issue is so important I suggest it may be worth your or your secretary's time to call as many past clients as possible and ask for their e-mail address. Moreover, I further recommend that you contact every potential referral source you can think of and get their e-mail address, as well. If mental health professionals, early in their practice, make it a custom to collect the e-mails of every new client and every potential source they meet, it will not be very long before their e-mail lists will be rather large.

Once you have a growing e-mail list of clients and (potential) referral sources you can do a number of important things: First, of course, you could more easily contact individual clients for one reason or another—missed appointment, check on their progress, note that you haven't heard from them in a while, or perhaps an insurance problem. Second, you could use the list to send out a periodic newsletter. (More on that later.) Third, you could send out announcements that you have completed new training, have recently written an article or a book, or you have been asked to speak somewhere in the near future. Fourth, once your e-mail list has become large enough, in addition to promoting an article, a book, or a new service (such as biofeedback or EMDR), you could also advertise a weekend retreat or a speaking series you plan to conduct. Obviously, an e-mail list comprised of past and present clients and referral sources is an excellent, powerful, marketing tool.

Collect through the window

The best time to collect the patient's money is either before or immediately after the session. Once a client leaves the office owing money, it will take significant time, effort, and some additional money to collect it. If you are dealing with Managed Care, you are already substantially discounting your fee. You, therefore, should not have to spend additional time and money to collect deductibles and co-pays. By collecting everything owed at the time of the service, there is no need to waste the time and money to send out bills to patients. I rarely do. A well-run office should collect better than 98% of the real fees owed.

Studies have shown that if the patient leaves without paying what they owe, there is substantial likelihood they will never pay the bill: If the bill is outstanding for more than 45 to 60 days, there is about a one in three chance you will not get paid. If the bill is outstanding 90 to 120 days, it is now about 50-50 that you will get paid. Accounts receivable that are nine months or more old have less than a one in four chance of being paid.

We work very hard for our money and we should get paid. I generally recommend against sending a patient to collection, as the agency gets about 50% of the money and the patient will likely thereafter speak badly about you. Also, there is a high incidence of clients filing malpractice claims against mental health providers once they are turned over to a collection service. Again, get all the money owed at the time of service and you greatly reduce the chance of having to chase the client for fees owed.

If I am unclear whether there is a deductible, for example, I will ask the client for the money at the time of the service. If, subsequently, I learn the deductible was, in fact, covered, I immediately reimburse the patient. I have said to many clients, "I don't want money to get in the way of treatment. Thus, I would prefer that I owe you rather than you owe me." If a client, for some reason, owes money, the bill should be sent immediately. If you wait 30 or more days to send out a bill you are likely to wait that long—or longer—to receive payment.

I do not know of any business today that does not take credit cards. Since your practice is a business, you absolutely should be set up to take credit cards. People today are quite comfortable paying with plastic and, as a business, we should accommodate them. Clients sometimes forget their checkbook or have used their last check, so they can pay you with a credit card. The credit cards also allow the clients to finance the payment, if they choose. The few percent the bank charges us is worth the added convenience.

Verify insurance

Insurance must be verified prior to the client's first session. To do so the necessary information needs to be gleaned—patient name, birth date, social security number, name of policy holder, and the policy holder's birth date and social security number. Some insurance plans are now using account numbers in place of social security numbers. The purpose of the verification is to determine if the insurance is valid, whether there is a deductible, what is the co-pay, and what are the restrictions, if any (such as 20 mental health sessions per calendar year—which is quite common in my area). In most cases, today, the verification can be done online.

The process must be done because most clients do not know this information. (In some cases, they may know it but prefer that you not know the information—such as in the case of a large deductible). If you proceed without verifying the insurance, you could find yourself having seen the client four to six times or more before you receive your first EOB (explanation of benefits) and learn the client has a $500.00 deductible that has not been met. The client paid you their small co-pay for each of the past several sessions but now you have to collect another $300.00 or more from them. This may not be easy and it likely will be time-consuming and expensive.

Confirm all appointments

Before my secretary leaves for the day, she calls and confirms (or leaves a message) regard the appointments for the next day. (On Friday she confirms Monday's appointments.) By this procedure I have salvaged hundreds of sessions over the years, as many clients have said that without the reminder call, they would have "forgotten" the appointment. This is especially true for clients that I see every two or three weeks. It is rare today that I see a client weekly over a long time. It is more common today for me to see clients every other week, so they may need a reminder.

Fairly often the client will say, upon receiving the confirmation call, "Oh, I was planning to call you and cancel that appointment." (What they really mean is that they were going to be a no-show/no-call.) This is particularly characteristic of new clients, unfortunately. By having this information you can manage your time more efficiently, instead of waiting for a client who is not coming. With this advance notice, you now have the opportunity to schedule another client in that slot. Knowing ahead of time a client is canceling is especially helpful when you have a waiting list—which I often do. Additionally, if you have a new patient scheduled a day or two or so away, you can call the new patient and see if they would like to come in sooner.

Since the cancellation and no-show rate is highest for new clients, the sooner you can get them in, the better. It has been my experience that if prospective new clients schedule their first appointment two to three weeks out, the odds are high they will subsequently cancel or no-show. The process of confirming appointments takes just a few minutes but it can save considerable money and allow for better use of your time.

50-minute hour

My sessions last 50 minutes. I use that spare 10 minutes in the hour to make a phone call, review the chart of the next client, or go to the bathroom. Many years ago I would take clients in on the hour and conclude at ten minutes to the next hour. My secretary occasionally reported that some clients complained that I had short-changed them. As an experiment, about a decade ago I began taking in clients at ten minutes after the hour and ended on the hour. I have not heard a complaint since.

Leave the door open when you terminate

Many times in my career when conducting an intake with a new client/patient, I learn the client has seen another mental health provider in the recent past. When I ask them why they did not choose to go back to that professional, I hear a lot of different responses, but, by far, the most common answer I receive is, "I didn't think I could or should."

After getting these responses for years I believe I have a sense of what is going on: The client thinks that when they see a mental health professional they are going to get a "total psychological house cleaning." If, at a later date they feel the need for some additional treatment, they are sometimes uncomfortable returning to that therapist because they feel somewhat embarrassed that they still have issues and they do not want to imply that the therapist was ineffective or did not do a complete job. After all, they think they already had a "total psychic overhaul" so they should not need to ever see a mental health professional again.

Whenever I terminate with a client, I ask them to consider me as their "primary care mental health provider." I relate to them that if they go in to see their family physician for a problem, say, stomach distress, they may see the physician for a few visits until the problem is solved. If they develop another problem, such as a headache, or even a re-occurrence of the stomach troubles, they should have no problems returning to their family physician for treatment. I suggest to the client that they should consider the treatment with me-their primary mental health provider—along those same lines. We have just dealt with this one issue, if the same one returns or a new one develops, they should feel no problems returning to me. I contend that if more therapists had this kind of conversation with their clients during the termination session, therapists would have more repeat business.

Additionally, if the treatment process went well, in the termination session I will note that I tend to work in a short-term, solution-focused manner, so I require a flow of new clients. Thus, if they were satisfied with their treatment, I welcome their referrals, if they choose to make them.

Remember, this is a business!

Important points to remember in CHAPTER FOUR:

1. Get e-mail addresses of every new client, all referral sources, and any old clients.

2. Collect through the window.

3. Verify insurance.

4. Confirm appointments.

5. Terminate treatment in a manner that makes more return business likely.

Action steps to take from CHAPTER FOUR:

1. Immediately alter your registration form to capture the clients' e-mail addresses.

2. Ask every client and current referral source for their e-mail address. Whenever you meet potential new referral sources, ask for their e-mail address, as well.

3. Have your staff call clients that have terminated (positively, of course) within the past year and request their e-mail addresses, telling them they will be able to receive your newsletter, or other important information. (This exercise will be more than worth the time as a number of clients will undoubtedly return.)

4. Review with your staff the importance of verifying insurance, confirming appointments, and collecting all monies owed before the client leaves the office.

5. Set up a credit card account to facilitate the ease of clients paying you.

6. Consider consulting with an experienced colleague regarding your practice.

Whatever we learn has a purpose and whatever we do affects everything and everyone else, if even in the tiniest way. Why, when a housefly flaps his wings, a breeze goes round the world; when a speck of dust falls to the ground, the entire planet weighs a little more; and when you stamp your foot, the earth moves slightly off its course. Whenever you laugh, gladness spreads like the ripples in a pond; and whenever you're sad, no one anywhere can be really happy. And it's much the same thing with knowledge, for whenever you learn something new, the whole world becomes that much richer.

Norton Juster, The Phantom Tollbooth

CHAPTER FIVE

PRACTICING WITH MANAGED CARE (MC)

History of Managed Care (MC)

I have been in the field long enough to have practiced before the advent of MC. When I began to practice in 1979 all insurance plans were referred to as "indemnity" plans. The client typically had a deductible, like $100.00, and the insurance paid 90% of the total bill, with the client paying the other 10%. After an out-of-pocket stop-loss of $1,000.00 was reached, the insurance plan paid 100%—to a lifetime maximum of one million dollars. Clients could see any licensed/certified provider of their choosing and their insurance would pay the bill.

MC began making its appearance in early- to mid-1980's. To my knowledge, the initial "hot spots" of MC were in the Twin Cities area of Minnesota, Phoenix, and Southern California.

Proponents of MC argued that health care costs in general were increasing far too quickly, comprising about 15% (then) of the nation's GNP and that doctors' fees, in particular, were out of control. MC was going to better regulate health care, curtail the spiraling cost of health care, manage the over-utilization of health care services, limit doctors' fees, and generally make health care more affordable and available.

By the late 1980's to early '90's MC had made major inroads in many of the larger cities. Phoenix was "penetrated" by better than 50% at that time; by the late '90's MC had "captured" better than 95% of the Phoenix market. MC was viewed as especially attractive initially by large employers because their cost to insure their employees was lower relative to indemnity plans—at least for a time.

To practice with a particular MC firm you had to join the "provider network"—that is, become a "member of the tribe," so to speak. By joining a provider network the provider agreed to abide by the provisions of that particular plan. The key component was to agree to accept a set fee for a session of psychotherapy. The arranged fee was often 30-40% less than the provider's standard fee. If you were not a member of the network, you could not get paid. As MC began to add more and more "lives" to their plans, providers felt increasing pressure to join plans, as they feared there would be fewer and fewer clients they could possibly see.

Initially, many MC firms in the mental health arena hired dozens of "case managers" to regulate the care. After three to six sessions with a client, depending on the plan, I would have to contact a case manager, discuss the case and the treatment plan, so the client could be "authorized" for an additional three to six sessions. Typically, as I had more sessions with a particular client, fewer and fewer authorized sessions were allowed before another "treatment review" with the case manager was required. Some plans hired their own clinical staff to work with the more difficult or needy patients.

Early on, if a client wanted service, he would call an 800 number, speak to an "intake representative" about his case, and be given a referral to a specific network provider in their zip code. The client usually paid a nominal co-pay ($5 or $10) and most often there was no deductible.

Presently, indemnity insurance is essentially a thing of the past, as MC completely controls our nation's health care. Case managers and treatment review sessions, thankfully, are also gone. Some plans still require that the client speak to an intake person and get a referral but many plans now allow the client to directly contact any provider in the network. Clients now often have hefty co-pays—$40-$50 is not uncommon—and often substantial deductibles also apply. With most plans, providers can bill on-line.

My History with Managed Care (MC)

In 1980 I was approached by a MC firm to help them train their "in-house" staff and become a "preferred provider." At that time, just a year or so into my private practice, my fee per session was $65.00. This company offered $75.00 per session and said that in short time they would be sending me lots of clients. Ten dollars more a session and I would not have to search for clients? How could I say no! (I didn't know it at the time, but I had just "made a pact with the devil"—but more on that later.)

I have since worked with MC for nearly 30 years. At one time I was "in-network" with about 10 companies. Today I work with three firms, soon to be two—and the original one referred to above is not one of them.

The benefit of working with Managed Care (MC)

The primary benefit of working with MC is, simply, that the company sends clients to you. As discussed previously, some MC firms allow their subscribers to contact the mental health provider directly and some require that the client contact the MC firm first and then is referred to a provider. In either case, the client comes to the provider—the provider does little, if anything, to get a patient.

When I began in practice in the late 1970's and early '80's it took a year or more before I had anything close to a full schedule. Today if a provider opens up a practice and is able to plug into a few MC firms which are active in his or her community, he or she could be fairly busy in a matter of months. Thus, the major (if not only) benefit of working with MC is that you can start your practice relatively quickly and possibly can maintain a fairly busy practice seeing MC clients.

Factors to consider before joining a MC company

There are a number of factors you should contemplate before you sign up to become a provider with a particular MC network:

1. Of course, what is the fee they will pay you? Whatever it is, it will probably remain for a long time.

2. Importantly, for me anyway: What is the ease of billing and what is the process used to correct a claim paid incorrectly (which you can bet will occur)? Aside from #1 above, this issue is critical. In the past I have left plans that paid more but could only be billed through an intermediary, and took much valuable time to correct their payment errors.

3. How many subscribers do they have or intend to have in your area? If there are too few "lives" in your area, it will not be worth your time to join the plan.

4. How many mental health providers do they intend to impanel. If they will invite and accept everyone in town, there probably will be not enough clients to go around.

5. How does the client get to you? I tend to prefer plans in which the subscriber must go through the intake department, since I will market to that department (as I will note just ahead). With a last name ending in W, many clients do not go all the way to the end of the network provider list. Now, if I can attach my website to that listing, then I will likely attract more clients.

6. How simple is the plan for clients to understand? I was once briefly a member of a plan that charged a separate deductible for mental health. My secretary and I were constantly having to explain this to those clients, as many of them did not understand their plan and assumed I was charging them an extra deductible.

7. How many sessions allowed and/or initially authorized? Clearly, the more, the better.

8. What is the process to reach a case manager or administrator if you have a problem? I have left plans where I had to call 2-3 times and wait days to get a response to a concern.

9. How easy is it to get the client to a psychiatrist or to the hospital? This will inevitably arise and the smoother the process the better.

Getting into Managed Care (MC)

A concern that some mental health providers have regarding MC is that they cannot become "impaneled." Some MC firms have so many providers they simply do not need or want any more. The exception to this is psychiatrists, as every MC firm will welcome a psychiatrist, most especially a child psychiatrist, as psychiatrists are in such short supply.

Though a MC panel may be closed to additional psychologists or therapists, experience has taught me there are several ways that you can get around this problem:

1. Do some research and learn the identity of some of the managers of that MC organization in your area. Once you get that information check around to see if you know someone who knows one of them. With the assistance of your contact putting in a good word for you, you probably will be able to get into the network.

2. Connect with a primary care provider, or especially a psychiatrist, who is already a network provider for that MC organization. Have him or her write that plan asking them to impanel you so that the provider can maintain a preferred referral pattern.

3. For several other tips on getting into closed panels, attend one of my seminars or go to MentalHealthMarketingAcademy.com.

Marketing with Managed Care (MC)

If you intend to work largely or exclusively with MC, your marketing efforts will be directed in three basic areas:

1. The MC mental health provider profile list
2. The MC intake office
3. Primary care providers (PCP's) who are in the same MC network

MC organizations have provider listings and descriptions on their websites and/or in their annual bulletins to which subscribers can refer. Some MC sites allow the providers to attach their own professional website. If you have a website—and you should!—by all means attach it. (For a professional, personalized website designed to attract clients in your particular area, click on www.MentalHealthMarketingAcademy.com.) If you do not have a website then carefully complete the MC provider information form. As noted previously, advertising evening and Saturday hours will certainly get you a lot of MC clients. My experience with MC clients is that hours and location are probably the two most important factors. (The truth is most MC clients select their therapists as if they were seeking a plumber—location, price, hours, or referred by their home warranty company. Interestingly, plumbers are usually listed on the same page as psychologists in most Yellow Pages.) Since I have a website, have offices in the northeast and northwest part of the Valley, and hold evening hours, I get a large number of MC calls.

If the MC plan operates such that clients must be referred by an "intake coordinator," then it makes good sense to get to know those people. If the intake office is located in your locale, then make arrangements to stop by, "meet and greet," and let them attach a face to the name, and discuss their problems and what kinds of cases with which you work.

If the intake office is located on the other side of the country, you can and should call the intake department as if you were a prospective client, and make a connection with the intake department in that manner. In either case, you should also establish a relationship with the managers in your area. If you make a good connection with the local management staff, you can ask that they put in a good word for you with the intake department.

Soliciting primary care providers (PCPs) is a critical part of marketing for mental health providers. If you are searching for MC clients, your "hook" is that you and that doctor are on the same plan, so it can be assured that patients can smoothly transition from their PCP to their mental health provider. If the PCP recommended you, the client will often contact you—if the plan provides for direct utilization of a specialist. If the plan requires that the client go through the intake office, if the client requests a particular provider (assuming that provider is in the network), the intake coordinator will almost always make that particular referral.

Marketing to PCP's will be discussed in greater depth in the section on marketing and developing a cash-pay practice. Moreover, most of the other suggestions in that section could also be used to procure more MC clients.

Import points to remember from CHATER FIVE:

1. The primary benefit of working with MC is that you do not have to search for clients, as they are sent to you.

2. Consider the various factors inherent in that MC plan before you join it.

3. You can enter a closed MC panel by connecting with a manager or by having a PCP or, especially, a psychiatrist, advocate for you to maintain their preferred referral pattern.

4. Your marketing targets with MC are the MC provider profile list, the intake department, and the PCPs and psychiatrists who also are providers in the network.

Action steps to take from CHAPTER FIVE:

1. Consult the list of medical providers in the network and identify the PCPs and psychiatrists located reasonably near you. Commit to meeting each one of them in the next 90-120 days.

2. Determine who are the administrators of the network in your locale and make a point of connecting with them.

3. An important question to ask such an administrator is in what specialty areas do they need more coverage? If any area is of any interest to you do some reading about it and attend a relevant workshop, and consult with a colleague to develop that specialty.

Doing is a quantum leap from imagining. Thinking about swimming isn't much like actually getting in the water. Actually getting in the water can take your breath away. The defense force inside of us wants us to be cautious, to stay away from anything as intense as a new kind of action. Its job is to protect us, and it categorically avoids anything resembling danger. But it's often wrong. Anything worth doing is worth doing too soon.

Barbara Sher

Don't wait for your ship to come in, swim out to it.

Source Unknown

CHAPTER 6

PROBLEMS WITH MANAGED CARE

Loss of Control

Ten or so years ago I conducted at least one or more psycho-educational evaluations a week. Currently, I perform such an evaluation about once a month, and sometimes even less often. It is not that such a procedure is no longer very useful or important; it simply is due to the fact that MC firms no longer cover such procedures.

Frequently, I have a case in which I believe it would be beneficial to assess the child's learning strengths and weaknesses, to rule out borderline IQ or slow learning, to rule out an attention deficit disorder or a learning disability, or to assist in determining why the child continues to earn poor grades. Although I am the professional, I am unable to manage the case as I see fit—if the client is associated with MC.

Many of my MC clients in Phoenix are limited to 20 outpatient sessions per calendar year—and they must be deemed "medically necessary" by the MC firm. This number includes any visits to a psychiatrist or any other mental health professional they may have seen that year. Moreover, if clients happened to stay a few days in a psychiatric facility (and a "few days" is all they are going to get—but more on that later) the number of remaining sessions could be rather few. Some cases could require weekly sessions for a time, or even twice-weekly visits. With only 20 available sessions per year, or possibly less, the therapist is under pressure to effectively treat clients in the few available remaining sessions. Although I am probably dating myself, I am reminded of the old quiz show "Name That Tune"—as "I can treat that patient in seven sessions, Bob."

I have been in the unfortunate position of taking on a patient with only a few sessions available for the year. Of course, you cannot "dump" a patient under those circumstances. You are ethically required to continue to treat that patient—while that client's MC firm has its policyholder treated for free.

I am reminded of the timely story in which three health care professionals approach the Pearly Gates before God. The first professional, a family practice physician, tells God that he has seen and helped thousands of patients with their medical problems during his career—and God welcomes him into heaven. The second professional, a psychotherapist, tells God that she has counseled hundreds of clients over the years, enabling them to ease their emotional pain—and God welcomes her into heaven. The third professional, a quality assurance nurse with a MC firm, tells God that during her career she has saved her company millions of dollars—and God welcomes her into heaven...but only for three days!

I have a number of clients who also see one of the psychiatrists in our office. To save on driving and for convenience, they commonly try to schedule to see me and their psychiatrist on the same day. Unfortunately, some MC plans will not pay for two mental health procedures on the same day, so the patient is not allowed that convenience.

MC sets the price, determines the allowable procedures, limits the number of sessions the professional can have with that patient, and will not allow the patient to see two mental health providers on the same day. It should be obvious, then, that any mental health professional who opts to work with MC gives up considerable professional control.

Also, the psychiatrists I work with frequently lament that MC essentially dictates what medications they can prescribe. They make the diagnosis but then consult the patient's particular MC formulary before they write out the prescription. I remember the days when insurance companies simply paid for health care—and still made a fortune at it. Today, MC controls health care—a classic case of "the tail wagging the dog."

Issues with privacy and confidentiality

Recently, a young man in his mid-twenties called me, upset. He related that he saw me when he was a pre-adolescent. He now is a successful young professional, recently married. As a responsible new husband, he decided to take out a life insurance policy. After applying and signing all the forms, the insurance underwriting department contacted him and said that since he was diagnosed with ADHD as a child, he was not eligible for preferred rates.

This individual thought I had done something wrong. How did his life insurance company know abut his childhood ADHD unless I told them? I assured him that that was not the case. I recommended to him that either he get a letter from his last provider or undergo a current evaluation to document that he no longer has any symptoms of ADHD. (Remember, you are always marketing.)

What this young man and most other individuals fail to appreciate is that every time an individual uses his health insurance—for anything—that information goes into a clearinghouse of insurance data which, I believe, is housed somewhere in Massachusetts. This clearinghouse serves most insurance companies, of all sorts, including life and disability, which can be tapped for past history, including pre-existing conditions.

Who has that information, and how many people can access it? How secure is it? For what else could that data be used? (In one of my last graduate classes I taught a student who had sold auto insurance for the past 15 years; she told the class that her company checks the credit rating of every individual before they offer a policy and was considering checking into the health database, primarily to learn of past or current problems with substances.)

As we all know too well, MC requires that we providers attach a DSM-IV diagnosis to every person we see. What will be the effect of providing a psychiatric diagnosis of almost any kind to a child's future? Given how easily information is disseminated today, and especially in the future, what will be the effect of attaching a diagnosis to anyone, for that matter?

MC obviously requires us to work within the "medical model." We have to diagnose every client—no, make that patient—with a DSM number so we can get paid. Thus, for a MC client to see us, they must be "ill." Where and when did it get written that therapists can only see "sick" people?

In my 30 years of practice I have had to write several letters for previous clients about their past treatment because they were seeking positions with various governmental agencies. I have also done numerous psychological evaluations over the years on private and commercial pilots when it has been discovered that they had once been given a mental health diagnosis and/or had been on psychotropics. (According to the FAA, you cannot fly a plane and be on Prozac at the same time. Apparently, it is better to fly untreated?)

Many MC plans require that the provider reveal more than the dates of service and diagnosis—"DOS and Dx," in insurance lingo. One of the MC firms I still work with asks that I provide a mini-survey for the client to take just before the first session and fax it to the company. (I find this so presumptuous. I have to greet the new client, have them complete my necessary registration material, and then have them fill out a survey—to provide the MC with more data. How much time does that leave me to conduct that all-important first session?)

Also, if you have seen a client, say, 15-20 times, this will probably trigger a computer alert and you may have to speak with a case manager to get additional sessions. In these case manager conferences the provider must offer more than the Dx and DOS. Furthermore, if your client requests short-term or especially long-term disability from work, most disability insurance companies request that you complete lengthy forms and forward the actual treatment notes. If your client does not authorize the release of that information, they will not receive any paid time off. Finally, some of the earlier MC plans I worked with have closed or were absorbed by other companies—which subsequently merged with other companies. What happens to the old information?

Some companies self-insure. They do the authorizing and have a contracted MC firm pay the health care provider. The DOS and Dx info, in this situation, goes to a department, usually associated with HR, in that company. What if that company's CEO wants to hire a new vice-president? After an exhaustive search and numerous interviews the CEO finally settles on two possible candidates for the job, both of whom already work within that company. Do you think it would be unreasonable to imagine that the CEO might want to take a look at the health care information that HR had on each of the candidates? If one of the candidates, say, had seen a mental health professional (or, on the other hand, had just been diagnosed with diabetes) what do you think would happen to that person's odds of securing that job?

In all of the above cases where does all this information go? Who has access to it? What is it used for? Ultimately, what happens to it? Confidentiality of health care records, in general, is important but, of course, is absolutely critical with respect to mental health records. Patient privacy and confidentiality, frankly, may not always be secure with MC.

I have had several cases where my clients, due to today's economy, were laid off from their job and decided to start their own business and/or become consultants. However, when they tried to purchase health insurance for themselves and their family, a pre-existing condition with them or a family member made the cost of the new coverage unreasonable. Thus, my clients were forced to seek other positions with large companies so they and their family could continue to receive health care—and they had to give up their dream of being their own boss.

Devaluing our service

Earlier in this book I spoke about valuing the services we provide. Mental health providers truly help people. We relieve people's emotional and physical pain. We teach them how to live better. We validate their concerns. We make a positive difference in people's lives. We save lives....

I believe the above with all my heart, because I have provided such services to patients for years. Nevertheless, the pragmatist in me forces me to accept the old adages: "You get what you pay for" and "It's only worth what someone is willing to pay." Therefore, when a client writes a check for a co-pay of 10 dollars for a treatment session, how much do they really value that hour? How likely is it they will follow up on the recommendations?

If, on the other hand, patients paid $125.00 (or more) for the session, would they likely value it more? Even more importantly, would they be even more willing to follow through with recommendations? I firmly believe the more the patients pay, the more they value the treatment. I believe that paying for the service is actually part of the therapy. It certainly has been my experience that I get far more late-cancellations and no-shows from my MC clients than I do from my cash-pay ones.

The point, of course, is that MC serves to devalue our service in the eyes of our MC consumers. Moreover, I contend that MC also causes many mental health providers to devalue their services to themselves, as well.

Addiction to MC?

As I noted previously, the one primary benefit of working with MC is that the client is sent to you; you do not have to solicit for your patients. At first, this may appear as a blessing. Over time, though, it becomes more of a curse because we get lazy and neglect to continue to market ourselves and our practice. Soon, we have lost our previous contacts and have become totally <u>dependent</u> upon MC to feed us—and are then unable to leave MC, even if we want to. Thus, if MC chooses to lower their fee, we have no choice but to accept it. (Isn't this a lot like how drug dealers operate?)

Crisis in Acute Care

Early in my practice I actively worked in psychiatric hospital settings. The typical length of stay (LOS) in the hospital then for a child was about 10 to 15 days; the average LOS for an adolescent was about 30 days; and the average LOS for an adult was about 10 days. We helped quite a number of people, then. We changed lives. We helped people get clean and sober—and stay sober—and get emotionally back on track.

Today, the LOS in most public psychiatric facilities is measured in hours—23 (yes, 23!), 48, and 72 hours are common for an in-patient stay. The goal for an acute care hospitalization today is "crisis stabilization." In other words, the object is to simply stabilize the patient—not really treat them.

Patients who overdosed and or cut their wrists and are deeply depressed are being discharged in 48 to 72 hours. Upon discharge they are referred to an outpatient therapist—which the hospital documents to cover their behind. How someone can be stabilized or helped in such a short time is beyond me.

Why has this happened in the past decade? Did our treatment methods become so much more effective? Has good research been conducted which proves that a two-to-three-day inpatient stay followed by outpatient treatment is more effective? The answer, of course, is no! The simple reason for the significantly reduced LOS in the acute care setting is that MC refuses to pay for longer stays.

When I discontinued inpatient work in the early 2000's there were about 300 psychiatric beds in the Phoenix metropolitan area. Today there are about half that many beds, as several facilities have closed. Since that time Phoenix has grown about 20 percent. The population in the "Valley of the Sun" did not get mentally healthier in the last decade, I do not believe. MC has simply chosen to no longer provide adequate acute care treatment. I believe the net result is that there is more crime, more homeless people, more people in shelters and on welfare, and more people in prison—but the MC executives are doing quite well financially, you can be assured. This crisis in acute care does present an opportunity, though—and more on that later.

Follow the money

Previously, I wrote that I had unknowingly made "a pact with the devil" when in about 1980 I signed on with the largest MC firm in the Valley; it is still the largest in town. That company offered me $75 dollars per session—which was ten dollars more than I was charging at the time. For a time, it worked. I saw lots of their clients. There was the occasional "lost claim" I submitted. Now and then I got stiffed when a client they referred subsequently was determined to not be an eligible subscriber for one reason or another (like lack of premium payments). I also got tired of the required case manager phone sessions that could only be held during regular working hours, which meant I had less available time to see clients.

Another significant concern working with MC was that with some companies the intake department and the claims department were in different cities, often in different states, and they did not communicate. A common problem I often run into occurs when a mother contacts the intake office and says she would like her child evaluated for ADHD or a learning disability, for example. Intake says go see Dr. Waldman. However, when I finally see Mother what she actually wants is psychometric testing—which I know the claims department will not cover. I am left with having to explain the situation to the parent. In some cases I have had the parent call intake back and specifically ask if psychometric testing for ADD or learning problems is covered, so they would believe me. In a few rare instances a cash testing case materialized.

Without a doubt, though, the most vexing issue was, over time, the fee they were paying was getting further and further away from my standard fee. As of this writing, my standard cash fee for an hour of psychotherapy is $125.00—$50.00 more than the average MC fee of $75 in Phoenix. That is a 40 % discount! Moreover, the average wait to receive payment for services rendered was 45-90 days.

In 2005 this large MC firm announced that a change in the fee structure was coming. Finally, I thought, I was going to get a raise after nearly 30 years of faithful service. The new fee turned out to be $73 dollars—two dollars less! That move showed me how much the firm valued my time—and I left them about a year later. (I called them and argued that I had been with them 30 years and had all that experience and thus deserved a raise. The response I received was that there were many providers who would be glad to accept their fee structure.)

If you ask any HR manager of any large company, "What has happened to your cost of insuring your employees with MC over the past two decades?" the answer, of course, you will receive is that the cost has continued to soar. If you ask any individual, "What has happened to your cost of insuring yourself and your family with MC over the past two decades?" the answer is always the same—the cost has continued to rise. Yet, if you ask any health care provider—GP, pediatrician, internist, surgeon, psychiatrist, psychologist, therapist, chiropractor, physical therapist, speech and language therapist—"What has happened to your remuneration from MC for your services over the past two decades?" the answer will be a resounding "It has gone down!" So, if the cost of health care to the employer and to the employee has continued to go up, and the fees paid to the providers have remained stagnant or gone down, where has all the money gone?!!!

I have a newspaper clipping in my desk drawer from 2007 about the CEO of a MC company, which is active in the Valley, who gave himself a bonus of 230 million dollars! (If anyone wants to give me a bonus, a half-million dollars will do just fine, thank you.) Two hundred and thirty million dollars would have paid every mental health provider in that network across the country a reasonable fee for their work that year!

I have since come to understand that the reason MC firms stopped using case managers to regularly monitor session usage was not because therapists became so prudent. MC cut back on the use of case management because they were making so much money charging today's inflated rates to consumers and paying 1980 fees for provider services, that there was little financial need to monitor us. Can you imagine a business in which you get to charge top of the market fees but pay your help 1980 wages—and you don't even have to provide employee benefits?!

The great irony is that MC initially promoted itself by saying they would reduce the rising fees being paid to doctors and manage the overall costs of health care. They certainly made good on the first promise: Most health care providers are making less today than 15 years ago or are working 40% harder to stay even. (Is there any wonder why your doctor is always behind and the waiting room is full?)

The second promise, though, regarding controlling the overall cost of health care, of course, is an abject failure. As already noted, the cost of health care has spiraled out of control, a large percent of the American public cannot even afford coverage, health care consumes more of our Nation's GNP than before the advent of MC (now about 17%), and the Federal Government is about to re-work the entire system. MC did not really intend to reduce the costs of health care; they planned to enrich themselves. MC simply re-distributed the money. Instead of thousands of health care providers receiving reasonable fees for their services, hundreds of MC executives have earned obscene fees for monitoring and <u>limiting</u> those services to millions of health care consumers. As far as I am concerned, MC has been the biggest boondoggle perpetrated on the American public since the Teapot Dome Scandal!

One area, though, I have to express admiration to MC for is their ability to market themselves. In less than a quarter century, MC was able to completely revamp our nation's health care system that had existed for decades. MC sold themselves to Government, Industry, and the People. Meanwhile, health care providers of all ilks sat idly by and let it happen. We health care providers should take note and pay much more attention to how we are perceived by Government, Industry, and the American Public.

Philosophical ruminations on Health Care

Please pardon me if I wax philosophical for a page or two.

I have auto and home owner's insurance. I was not thrilled to purchase these insurance plans but I was required to do so. It is the law in Arizona, and in most other states I presume, that if you choose to drive a vehicle, you must purchase auto insurance. By the same token, if you want a mortgage, it is mandatory that you have a home owner's policy—and the premium is even tacked directly onto the monthly mortgage payment. The cost of my auto insurance is not standard. The fee is contingent upon a number of variables: The make and model of the car or cars I drive; how many cars I have; how expensive they are; how old the car is; how expensive it is to fix; where I live; how many previous tickets I have had; how many accidents and claims I have had; whether there has been a DUI; and with which insurance company I choose to use. Similarly, the cost of my home owner's plan is also based on several factors: The size of the house; what it is constructed of; where it is located; how many previous claims I have filed; and, again, with which company I choose to do business. No one buys these insurances for me; I must pay for them myself.

Now consider health care insurance:

1. It is not mandatory.

2. We expect our employer to purchase it for us.

3. If we are not employed, we expect our government to provide it for us, for free.

4. We are forced to accept the one plan our employer or the government chooses for us.

5. We expect the traditional family of father, mother, and two children to pay the same premium as a family of father, mother, and six children.

6. We expect someone, who, say, is 50 years old, who works out, watches his or her weight, eats correctly, and does not smoke, to pay the same for personal health insurance as someone, also 50, who never exercises, is 60 pounds overweight, eats poorly, and smokes one-and-one-half packs of cigarettes a day.

How did it happen that we developed such different expectations regarding health care insurance relative to other forms of insurance? When did we become so entitled? Is it any wonder why our health care system is in such a mess?

I believe that health care insurance ought to operate much like auto insurance:

1. Health care insurance be required by law.

2. Employers can pay their employees more because they are not paying for health care benefits.

3. If individuals are unemployed, they may choose a plan but it is paid for from unemployment benefits.

4) There are many plans and programs from which to choose, which will increase competition and lower the cost of insurance.

5. Individuals choose the coverage and deductibles that are right for them, above the mandated minimum.

6. The individual can change plans, like we can change auto insurances, if a better plan becomes available.

7. The cost of the plan is contingent on individual variables—number of persons in the family and specific health factors, which will reward people who are conscientious concerning their health.

I contend that this kind of program, or one like it, emphasizes personal responsibility—which is sadly lacking with respect to health care. In addition, as a health care provider, if the average individual takes health care for granted and makes only a nominal co-pay to obtain health care service, they are likely to not value that service very much—as described previously. If people are allowed to exercise more choices and be more responsible with their health care coverage, they will likely more highly value the treatment they receive. It would be nice for hard-working, dedicated health care providers to once again receive the respect and financial consideration they lost through MC about a quarter-century ago.

Within the past 25 years MC significantly reduced the income of all health care providers and, at the same time, greatly limited the health benefits of millions of Americans. Moreover, MC also changed the fundamental Zeitgeist with respect to how health care is provided. Before MC, money essentially was exchanged when treatment was provided. Insurance companies, then indemnity type, made money through premiums paid by employer and by the employee, and saved money by the substantial deductibles and co-pays paid by the patients when they sought treatment.

Today, MC earns essentially all their income from the premiums paid by the employer and the employee. The co-pays are insignificant. Thus, the money to MC is pre-paid. Providing treatment now represents a significant cost—most especially with the HMO model. The bottom line, then, is that 25 years ago health care operated on a fee-for-service basis; today, MC makes money not by providing care but by restricting it—a complete paradigm shift.

It is basic psychology and human motivation. If you can make money by providing services, you will provide services. If, on the other hand, you make money by withholding services, you will withhold services. Most consumers fail to understand that their health care provider makes more money by restricting services than by providing them. I have had numerous cases where I have urged patients to strongly advocate for themselves or for a family member and have ultimately obtained treatment that had been previously denied.

While writing this I came upon this article in the Arizona Republic, dated Wednesday, July 22, 2009:

"HealthNet will sell its Northeast business to United Health Group for about five hundred and ten million dollars but keep its Arizona unit because of the local operation's improved financial results." (They earn five hundred and ten million dollars but we health care providers have to work with a 40% discount!) The article goes on to say that the "firm's local operation earned a pre-tax profit of more than four million dollars during the first three months of the year (2009) but had a more difficult year last year. (Four million dollars in the first quarter and they are complaining?!) 'We were hit with the flu last year,' the President said." (As just discussed, it used to be that insurance companies made money when people got sick but clearly this is no longer the case.)

Also while writing this book, there was much talk circulating about universal health care. The concept of the Government running our health care system scares me almost as much as the current MC system. How are the Post Office, Amtrak, and Social Security alike? They are all run by the Government and they are all almost bankrupt! If you think that MC has been paying us too little for our service—as I certainly do—you are likely to become really upset when you learn what the Federal Government intends to pay us for a session of psychotherapy. As of this writing, Medicare has proposed to lower our fees by about 30%.

Recently, the "Cash for Clunkers" Government program to stimulate auto sales concluded and it has become known that car dealerships are complaining loudly that they are not receiving their rebates from the Government. If auto dealers cannot get their $4,500.00 rebate per car sold from the Government, how hard would it likely be for us to get our few dollars back from the Government for a session of psychotherapy?

What can you realistically expect to earn with a MC practice?

Let's consider a busy psychologist who runs a MC practice. The average fee per session from MC in Arizona—though it varies by locale—is about $75. A psychologist, conservatively speaking, if fairly busy, can see on average about 30 clients per week. Given time off for a vacation, holidays, and for conferences, most clinicians might work 48 full weeks a year.

So let's do the math: $75 times 30 clients per week times 48 weeks per year equals $108,000.00. A master-level therapist generally receives about 15 percent less from MC than a Ph.D.-level psychologist, so the yearly income for a therapist or counselor with a MC practice would be about $90,000.00.

Now at first blush 108K or 90K sounds like a decent income. It is a living. But let's look a bit more closely: Office rent is about $1,000.00 per month. Your share of the secretary is also about $1,000.00 per month. Phone, electricity, water, supplies, lease on the copier, office cleaning, and maintenance could equal $750.00 per month. Billing services are approximately $250.00 per month. Professional liability and the required continuing education run about another $250 per month. And since you are working privately, let's not forget the cost of your and your family's health care insurance of about $500 per month (conservatively speaking). I have not yet mentioned any costs associated with purchasing the fax machine and buying all the furniture necessary for an office, but you could easily tack on another couple of hundred dollars a month. So, again, let's do the math: $1,000.00 (rent) plus $1,000.00 (secretary) plus $750.00 (expenses) plus $250 (billing) plus $250.00 (liability and CE) plus $500.00 (health insurance) all times 12 (months), equals about $45,000.00.

So, if we take 108K or 90K and subtract the cost of doing business of about 45K, that leaves a net profit of about 63K or 45K, respectively. Then, let us not forget, we must pay taxes on those net figures. Moreover, what about putting some money away each month for retirement?

Now for those of you who choose to work within this situation, I say "God bless you." Frankly, though, it is a lot of stress and hard work for what I consider to be relatively little financial reward.

My younger son, Chad, has decided to go into my field. I know him well. He has many, many fine qualities but he is clearly not an entrepreneur, marketing person, or business person. Therefore, I have encouraged him to become a school psychologist—which is how I started out.

Chad will earn 50K-60K a year, for 10 months. In addition, he will have considerable time off; he will be home by dinnertime; he will not have any emergency calls; he will have his health insurance, professional liability insurance, and continuing education paid for; and he will earn a pension when he retires. Frankly, on balance, Chad will earn as much or more than most clinicians in a MC practice—with far less stress.

Now, if we can alter the above financial formula and change that $75 per session (or $65 for a therapist) to $125, or more, things begin to look much brighter. When I am involved with a legal case, for example, I can earn upwards of $250 per hour—cash, up front. When you can earn at that rate, all your hard work and training is appropriately compensated. Therefore, the remainder of this book will be devoted to developing a cash-pay practice.

Important points to remember in CHAPTER SIX:

1. Problems with MC include reduced income, loss of professional control, concerns about confidentiality, and the devaluing of our service.

2. MC has not kept its promise to manage health care.

3. With a MC practice a busy psychologist can expect to earn a net yearly income of 63K and a busy therapist about 50K.

Action steps to take from CHAPTER SIX:

1. Commit to writing articles and/or generating media interviews to alert the public about the problems with our current health care system.

2. Recognize what you can earn with a MC practice and vow to take full advantage of every available working hour.

Are you in earnest? Seize this very minute! Boldness has genius, power, and magic in it. Only engage, and then the mind grows heated. Begin, and then the work will be completed.

John Anster

You must take action now that will move you towards your goals. Develop a sense of urgency in your life.

Les Brown

CHAPTER SEVEN

DEVELOPING A CASH-PAY, FEE-FOR-SERVICE, PRACTICE

All or Nothing?

Developing a cash-pay practice requires a commitment on the part of the therapist to leave the "safety" of MC. (Given all the issues associated with MC, though, as discussed previously, it may be strange to refer to working with MC as "safe.") Nevertheless, there undoubtedly is some allure to having clients come to you automatically. Running a cash-pay practice means you must work harder to procure your clients/customers and discontinue your reliance on MC to "spoon-feed" you clients.

"Cutting the cord" with MC can be frightening. But it does not have to be done all at once. It can be done gradually.

I mentioned earlier that I once belonged to nearly a dozen MC firms. Over the years I have sifted through them and presently I work with just two firms—and one of them (Blue Cross Blue Shield—BC/BS—of Arizona, my favorite)—operates more like an indemnity plan. I "fired" the other plans because they were difficult to work with, it was maddening to correct a billing problem, they paid too little (BC/BS pays the best—which is why they are my favorite), they covered too few lives in the Valley so it was not worthwhile to remain with them, or my practice became busy enough that I no longer needed or wanted them.

An interesting event occurred with most of the plans after I left them. As many of us know, MC firms are quite slow in updating their records. Thus, after I resigned from a plan I continued to get patients referred from that plan—especially if that plan allowed the client to contact the mental health provider directly and did not have to go through the intake process. I also found that some intake departments were also rather slow in getting updated, as well. When such a client called, my secretary, of course, informed them that I was no longer associated with that plan, but "as a special service to such clients, Dr. Waldman has a discounted cash fee that is available." We were able to convert about one out of four such callers to cash-paying clients—albeit at the discount. This demonstrates the "power of the referral"—but more on that in a bit. To this day, I still get calls from clients in plans that I left years ago. It is a strange twist of fate, but some MC plans actually helped me to develop my cash-pay practice.

With the two plans I have kept, plus all the other fee-for-service "irons I have in the fire," I keep very busy. The bulk of my income—about 70%, currently—comes from outside of MC. Within a year or so I intend to work only with BC/BS—unless they choose to lower their rates like the other plan did I noted previously.

I suggest you take a long look at the plans to which you belong. Decide which plan or plans would be the first to go, for many of the reasons I noted above. As you begin to market your cash-pay practice and receive some cash-paying clients, you can gradually resign from the least desirable plans. Over time, you will have a predominately cash-pay practice.

My colleague and partner with me in the building has had an entirely cash-pay practice for years. While he may not be as busy as I am (seeing patients), he earns probably more than I do. The fee from one of his cash-paying clients equals the fee from two and one-half of my MC clients. Thus, he works less, has less stress, has no billing costs (as cash-pay patients pay as they go), has no billing hassles with MC, and has the satisfaction of being paid in full immediately after every session—so there is immediate gratification. (It has always struck me as odd that when we finally receive that check from the MC firm we get excited—for getting money that was owed to us for our very hard work which we did for a 40% discount!)

Where did it get written that a MC client has to have the most-desired hours? I don't know, so I don't do it. As we all know, the late afternoon, early evening appointments are typically the most desirable or sought after. When I or my secretary reschedules cash-paying clients, they get whatever hour they want. I will not schedule a 4, 5, or 6 p.m. with an MC client until a day or two before it looks like I will not otherwise be able to book a cash-paying patient in that time slot. Frankly, when MC clients call to schedule their first appointment and they say they can only be seen at 5 or 6 p.m., my secretary has been instructed to tell them that I cannot accommodate them. (I got this idea from hotels that will not honor certain discounts until 30 or even 15 days before the desired stay. They, of course, would prefer to book a room at their standard rate, but as time draws near they are more willing to take a discounted rate. Remember, your practice is a business.)

My Survey

In preparation for this book I conducted a survey in May 2009 of psychologists who belong to AzPA—the Arizona Psychological Association. Approximately 550 psychologists were surveyed and about 80 responded. This response rate of approximately 18 percent, I have been told, is excellent in the survey world. The following is a review of the questions that were asked, the responses received, and some of the more significant comments offered at the end of the survey:

(The percentages are rounded)

1. What percentage of your clients comes from managed care sources?

Hundred percent	10%
About seventy-five percent	23%
About half	10%
About twenty-five percent	14%

None	43%

(Because Phoenix is such a competitive market, about 40% of the psychologists in this sample do not depend on MC for their clients but about 60% do. For about a third of the sample, they are almost exclusively dependent on MC.)

2. How would you rate the sources of new clients on a scale of 1 to 5 (where 5 is the most important source)?

	1	2	3	4	5
MC	42%	11%	14%	17%	16%
Client Referrals	7%	6%	29%	26%	3%
Referrals From Health care Professionals:	6%	7%	27%	18%	42%
Referrals From Other Sources	12%	20%	24%	22%	21%
Advertising And Marketing	53%	19%	9%	7%	12%
Other	52%	15%	7%	3%	3%

(Not surprisingly, client referrals and referrals from other health care professionals are seen as the most important referral sources.)

3. Would you like to increase the number of private, fee-paying clients?

Yes 80%

No 20%

(Surprisingly, 20% of this sample said they are not interested in increasing the number of cash-paying clients?)

4. Are you currently taking any action to increase your number of private, fee-paying clients?

Yes 43%

No 56%

(Interestingly, but not unexpected, nearly 60% are doing nothing to increase the number of cash-paying clients.)

5. Which of these marketing activities, if any, do you currently engage in?

Networking	83%
Public Speaking	45%
Article or book writing	23%
Direct Mail	6%
Yellow Page Advertising	25%
Print Advertising	9%
Radio or TV Appearances	6%
Online Marketing	29%

(Networking and public speaking is what most of these psychologists do for marketing; a sizable number are also online.)

6. Do you actively seek referrals from health care professionals or other professionals such as attorneys, etc.?

Yes 56%

No 42%

(About one-half of the sample do not seek referrals outside of health care.)

7. Do you have a practice website?

Yes 32 %

No 67%

(I find it surprising that about two-thirds of the sample do not have a website.)

8. If you have a website how many clients does your website bring you each month?

None	13%
One or two a month	24%
Several a month	11%
I have no website	51%

(Nevertheless, despite a larger number than expected having a website, these sites rarely bring in a client.)

9. Do you have a blog?

Yes 1%

No 99%

(Essentially no psychologist in AZ is blogging.)

10. Are you currently on Twitter?

Yes 5%

No 95%

(The same is true for Tweeting)

11. Do you have a professional presence on any social network websites like LinkedIn or Face Book?

Yes 24%

No 76%

(About one-quarter of the sample have a presence on a social network.)

12. How many hours would you say you spend each month on practice growth?

None	45%
One to two hours	37%
Three or more hours	19%

(Better than 80% of the sample spends two hours or less a month on marketing their practice.)

13. What percentage of your revenues do you reinvest in growing your practice?

Zero %	38%
1 to 5 %	39%
5 to 10 %	16%
More than 10%	7%

(Nearly 40% of the sample does not spend a dime on marketing.)

14. Which of these steps, if any, have you taken to help you grow your practice?

Read books or articles on practice growth	42%
Attend a seminar	26%
Take an online course	6%
Consult a marketing professional	13%
Work with a business coach	1%
No steps like these	51%

(Reading books—like this one—and attending a seminar—like mine—are the primary ways these psychologists learn about practice development.)

15. How satisfied are you with the revenues your practice produces today?

Totally satisfied	16%
Quite satisfied	57%
Not very satisfied	24%
Totally unsatisfied	3%

(About three-quarters of this sample were happy with the state of their practice, where one-quarter of this sample were clearly not.)

16. How confident are you about your long-term financial future and retirement?

Extremely confident	12%
Quite confident	57%
Not very confident	24%
Very concerned	7%

(About two-thirds of this group were confident regarding their future.)

Here are a number of the more significant comments the respondents made:

"I need more self-paid clients, no doubt about it."

(Most of us would agree.)

"I need to become more active in promoting my primary practice in creating a passive income stream that is practice-related."

(We will talk more about passive income.)

"I worry about psychologists advertising on places like My Space, etc. I think people should come to you by word of mouth and not advertising other than the traditional name, type of practice, and location. A web space is okay, if done professionally. We are not cars and look what happened to GM and Chrysler. I know I'm swimming upstream here but we need to be careful."

(Careful—of what? Becoming successful? It is time we get off our high—but poor—horse.)

"There is another side to practice of psychotherapy which is in the business arena. I can't help thinking if I wanted to be a business major, I would have gotten my MBA."

(You are not alone.)

"I should do a lot more to market myself.

(No question.)

"I wish practice building and marketing had been taught in graduate school. At the end of the day I do not have much energy left for marketing."

(Hence, the title of my book. The energy issue is a common theme.)

"I realize that I like to make more money but that I don't like asking patients for more money! Billing for insurance and requesting a modest co-pay is much easier. I believe this is largely due to my empathy for and awareness of financial struggles and the resulting difficulty paying one hundred dollars a week for treatment. Somehow, in my distorted mind, I perceived that paying cash for treatment shifts it from medically necessary treatment to an indulgence or luxury. What's up with that? I guess all that community mental health experience has me stuck in the social service model!"

(As I noted earlier, some of us cannot get away from the non-profit model. This psychologist also has an issue, I believe, with valuing his service. Lastly, who says our services have to be "medically necessary"?)

"Somebody forgot to provide a class in grad school on the business side of psychology. In order to be a successful behavioral professional it is necessary that one be business savvy, know something about marketing, and be a competent clinician."

(Again, that is exactly why I wrote this book.)

"Personally, I have some ethical concerns about psychologists (and other professionals) who seek more "private, fee-paying" patients—if this means the psychologist does not accept insurance coverage. What small socio-economic slice of society does this psychologist see?"

(Ethical concerns?! What is unethical about seeing clients that value your service? The answer to this psychologist's question is: committed, caring, dedicated patients who have concerns about privacy and outside control—and aren't always rich.)

The survey in general indicates, I believe, psychologists in Phoenix, due to the competitive nature of that market, are probably a bit more advanced in general marketing than many mental health professionals elsewhere. Nevertheless, the issues they are facing in Phoenix are universal. What to do about marketing, how to do it, and having the time, money, and energy to do it are common concerns. The survey also tapped the "holier-than-thou" mentality many providers have about marketing. I refer to those professionals as arrogant—and poor.

Market! Market! Market!

Recently I met a young psychologist at a conference and had a nice conversation. At the end of our chat I offered him my business card and asked him for his. He said he did not happen to bring any of his cards with him. Come to a conference without any business cards! I couldn't believe it! When I attend a professional conference, in my attaché case are my business cards, brochures, and several copies of my books. I view attending conferences as not only a method to obtain CEs and perhaps learn something, but also an opportunity to re-connect with colleagues and network with new ones. Remember, you are <u>always</u> marketing. Everyone you meet is a potential client or referral source.

A common problem most psychotherapists have with respect to marketing is finding the time—and energy—to do it. What we do can be exhausting. After a full day of seeing clients it can feel too taxing, for example, to carve out time to meet with a potential referral source for dinner or speak to the Parent-Teacher Organization (PTO) at a nearby school. The point, of course, is that we really have little choice. If we fail to market our practice, over time our referral sources may retire, die, leave town, or forget us and our practice will stagnate. While we certainly need to take time for ourselves, at the same time we must devote some time and effort—on a fairly regular basis—to maintaining and marketing our practice.

How are accountants, attorneys, architects, financial planners, chiropractors, and dentists alike? They all provide professional services and generally operate on a fee-for-service basis. These professionals have essentially functioned and flourished on a cash-pay business model for decades. If these professionals can do it, why can't mental health professionals?

Recently, an attorney friend of mine quipped that I was fortunate that people can use insurance to pay my bill. I answered I did not feel so fortunate. I indicated that, in fact, I envied his profession because attorneys largely rejected pre-paid legal services and have managed to maintain an expectation of fee-for-service.

Dentists and chiropractors are especially of interest because they provide health care. While some dentists and chiropractors accept insurance, the majority do not. Also, the insurance plans for dentists are not nearly so restrictive or financially limiting as the type of plan with which mental health providers must cope. (I am not that familiar with how MC treats chiropractors but I do know many plans do not cover that service—which, in my view, is in the best interests of chiropractics.) Dental plans may cover certain procedures but they often do not dictate to the doctor how much they can charge or receive for that work. Like the attorneys, the field of dentistry has controlled the insurance companies. On the other hand, the mental health field has succumbed to the power of MC. If other professionals can operate on cash, we should strive to do it as well.

Market to the masses—not just the sick

What percent of the U.S. population has a genuine psychiatric disorder—10%, 15%, 20%, 25%? By and large this is the population most mental health professionals market to—the sick, pardon the expression, portion of the population. We mental health professionals, therefore, are all fighting over the same small piece of the pie.

On the other hand, what portion of the population could benefit from some counseling, advice, and coaching with respect to parenting, marriage, stress management, wellness, effective communication, life transitions, and so on? One hundred percent!!

The entire population could and should avail themselves of these services.

Thus, it makes good sense that mental health professionals should not just focus on the smaller "ill" portion of the population but, instead, market to the larger "non-sick" segment. I contend that the field of mental health would be so much better off in general if we could convince more people to get away from the notion that one has to be "sick" or "crazy" to see a therapist. By reaching out to the larger, healthy portion of the population, we clearly increase our odds of securing more "clients"—not patients. From a marketing standpoint, then, it makes great sense to promote our services to the larger healthy segment of the population. I believe the field of coaching has made real inroads in this direction—and more on that later.

Solutions—not esoteric procedures

Whenever I travel I like to glance at the psychology section in the local Yellow Pages directory. Now, I want to go on record that I believe Yellow Page ads are a waste of money. They are quite expensive and you are committed to that expense for a year—even if you close your practice in the interim. It is my experience that Yellow Page ads rarely, if ever, attract enough new clients to pay for the monthly cost. Moreover, Yellow Page ads, I contend, are used primarily by "shoppers" who will go down the columns and call every psychologist or therapist who has an ad—"stealing" these therapists' time. Finally, the kind of client who is garnered through the Yellow Pages is not likely to be a dedicated one. I have not had an ad in the Yellow Pages for nearly two decades and it has not negatively affected my practice one bit.

Recently, I was in Laguna Beach, California and saw this impressive Yellow Page ad. It was impressive only because of its size—one column wide by about five inches long. I would not be surprised if the monthly cost of that ad approached $1,000.00. This psychologist noted the population he served and then listed the areas he addresses: depression, anxiety disorders, posttraumatic stress disorder, OCD, addictions, and personality disorders. Finally, he reported the services he provides—cognitive-behavioral therapy, biofeedback, NLP, EMDR, psycho-analysis, and family therapy.

Now for whom was this written? Obviously, this psychologist wrote this ad for the local population to attract local clients/patients. Yet, how many laypersons would look at this ad and know what most of it meant? How many people know the difference between cognitive-behavioral therapy and psycho-analysis, or between NLP and EMDR—or even care? Moreover, upon reading the ad the perspective clients might have to ask themselves, "Do I have an anxiety disorder? Or am I personality disordered?"

Mental health professionals write marketing copy and, very importantly, speak to potential clients, as if they read the DSM. Essentially, most mental health professionals engage in marketing that only other mental health professionals understand!!

I recommend that we must learn to speak in terms of the solutions we provide rather than the esoteric procedures we offer. For example, instead of saying I offer "parenting training," I tell people "I help parents learn how to more effectively teach their children to behave in a more responsible and less oppositional manner." In place of "marital therapy," I say "I teach couples to interact in a more positive, mutually-rewarding manner." In the above examples—and I could give you many more—the average "man or woman on the street" has a fairly good idea of the services I offer and can relate to the ultimate solution that, hopefully, can be achieved.

In marketing parlance, what I have just described is often referred to as the "elevator pitch." In other words, if you were in an elevator and someone standing next to you asked you what you did, could you answer that question before that person got off at the next floor? We all need to perfect our elevator pitch—one to three sentences that succinctly describes—in non-technical, observable, terms—what we do.

So, in light of the above discussion and the previous discussion about what perspective clients really find important, if I were to be so foolish as to have a Yellow Page ad, it would look something like this:

Larry F. Waldman, Ph.D., ABPP

Licensed Psychologist

11020 North Tatum Blvd., Suite 100
Phoenix, AZ 85028

(Located on Tatum, just north of Shea, conveniently situated between the 51 and 101)
Phone: 602-996-8619

Evening and Saturday (if I was 20 years younger) Hours Available

30 Years Experience

Diplomate from the American Board of Professional Psychology (ABPP)

Author of *Who's Raising Whom?*, *Coping With Your Adolescent*, and *How Come I Love Him But Can't Live With Him?*

Population Served:

Children, adolescents, adults, parents, couples
Services Offered:

Helping parents to teach their children to behave more responsibly and compliantly

Teaching couples to interact in a more positive, mutually-rewarding manner

Helping people with tension to relax and learn to overcome their fears

Conducting psychometric testing with children and adults to rule out problems with learning and/or attention and determine the individual's learning strengths and weaknesses

Conducting family studies to assist the Court in determining appropriate child custody arrangements

I specialize in short-term, problem/solution-focused treatment.

Insurance plans accepted:

BC/BS, United Behavioral Health, Health Net

I also have reasonable cash-fee rates.

For more information see: TopPhoenixPsychologist.com

To Schedule an Appointment call: 602-996-8619 and speak to Mia

In addition to the active solutions offered, written in understandable terms, notice that the other information included in the ad is of particular interest to prospective clients—location, hours, years of experience, insurances accepted, "reasonable" cash-fees, and "short-term treatment." (Most individuals have no idea what the ABPP is, but it sounds impressive.) Remember, as noted previously, many people choose their psychotherapist much like they would select their plumber when they have a plugged drain.

Keep in mind what is significant to you and your customer when you write marketing copy. Marketing copy should be concise, free of psychobabble, and easily understood by the average adult with a high school education. Also, note that my website is available for additional information.

The power of the referral

If you are going to develop a cash-pay practice, you will undoubtedly have to generate referrals. Although it may happen on occasion, it is most unlikely that scores of clients will come to you directly, on their own, and pay you cash. If you want to have a successful cash practice you will need a steady stream of referred clients.

A referred client is much more willing and likely to pay cash. If, for example, the pediatrician tells Mother that for years she has sent all her patients to Dr. Smith, psychologist, and the pediatrician has heard nothing but the most positive comments from her patients about Dr. Smith, Mother will very likely be highly motivated to take her child to Dr. Smith. In fact, even if Mother belongs to a MC network and Dr. Smith only takes cash, Mother still is likely to work with Dr. Smith because the pediatrician made that referral.

Though I have often said most people select their therapist like they choose their plumber, if they have a referral from a trusted source, they will seek that provider—and that plumber, as well. A solid referral base, then, is the life blood of a successful cash-pay practice.

Become the expert

Experts in sales and marketing often say, "The marketing begins before you say hello." Accordingly, if you develop a positive, professional name and reputation in your community, you will have a much better chance of securing an audience with a potential referral source and developing a referral relationship. In addition, if you become known as an "expert" in your community, there is high probability that patients will directly seek you out—and pay you cash to be seen by you.

There are a number of ways you can work to become known as "The Expert:"

1. Write articles. I am certain there have been many times that something in the news caused you to think, "I should write an article about that." I have thought that, too, and followed through with an article on numerous occasions. I tend to submit my articles to a local, weekly journal. Of course, you could submit your articles to the major local newspaper. I have written about effective studying, mental health care, the health care insurance situation (no surprise, there), making the best use of parent-teacher conferences, the problems associated with video gaming, our State's priorities with respect to education, and so on. I cannot say that the articles have brought me many cash-paying patients, though they have led to a number of clients. I believe the articles have reinforced my image as a well-written, thoughtful, experienced mental health professional in the community. Rarely a week passes by without some client, colleague, referral source, or friend, making reference to one of the articles I have written.

2. Make contact with reporters. If you notice an article in the newspaper or local magazine (as some communities have their own magazines) and you think you could provide a cogent comment, contact that reporter and indicate such. That contact could lead to a follow-up article, you could get interviewed, or, at the very least, the next time that reporter works on a psychologically-related issue, he or she will probably contact you—and you will get quoted, again, in the local media.

3. Write a book. Nothing labels you faster as an expert than becoming an author. We have all heard the cryptic phrase, "An expert is someone with a

> briefcase who is 50 miles or more away from home." I believe another definition of an expert is, "Someone who takes the time and effort to put their ideas in a book format."

Writing a book almost automatically gives you credibility and gets you in the door of referral sources. The book will get you interviews, speaking engagements, and clients—willing to pay you cash. A copy of a book is also something you "can leave" with a referral source when you meet them. Leaving a book is so much more powerful than a simple business card.

Importantly, a book can provide "passive income." Passive income is money that is earned without you having to directly work for it. (Remember the elements of an optimal business, discussed earlier.) This is something most mental health professionals know little about, as was noted earlier, because we typically only make money when we and our client are in the room at the same time. Once you have completed the effort of writing and developing a book, the work is essentially done. Any funds you receive after that is money earned without having to do additional work for it—hence, "passive" income.

I will not tell you that I have gotten rich with my four books, but I will tell you (and the IRS) that I have made about $50,000.00 over the years, which is a good return on my time investment (ROI—in business lingo).

My books are displayed in my office and weekly I sell a handful of them to individuals in the waiting room. I will also sell them, at a discount, to my clients to reinforce the therapy. The books are available to other psychotherapists as "bibliotherapy." Of course, I always have them available when I conduct seminars.

With today's word processing technology, it is fairly easy to write a book. The difficult part, of course, is gathering and developing the material, organizing it, and finding the time to write it. I always keep a yellow pad with me in my briefcase. If I happen to have an open hour, I use that time to work on the manuscript.

Getting a publishing house to produce your book is rather difficult today. Publishers are watching their pennies and, it seems to me, are reluctant to take risks on a new or unknown author. If you want to go the way of having your book published by a major publishing house, you will first need to secure a literary agent.

Literary agents will package and propose your book to a publisher. It is next to impossible today to get a manuscript even looked at by a publisher, much less adopted, if it is not sent through an agent.

Unless you happen to know a literary agent, you can attempt to find one through the Internet. There are several sites on which agents advertise. Of course, you will want to identify one that has had experience with representing a book on your topic. If you find an agent that seems like a good fit, contact him or her.

Another way to locate an agent is to go through a book store and see if there is a recently-published book that is in the same genre as yours that seems fairly well done. You can then contact the publisher or the author and ask who the agent was and proceed to contact him or her.

The advantage of having a book published is that you have professionals who edit the book and put it together. The biggest advantage is that the publisher has the funds and resources—should they choose to use them—to distribute and market the book. If you ever get so far as to begin discussing marketing strategies with a publisher, insist upon a marketing program that involves you going on tour and ensure such is written into the actual contract. For some publishers, marketing your book may only consist of simply placing it in a catalogue.

One of the disadvantages of having a book published by a major house is that you may lose some artistic and content control. (If you work with MC, you should be accustomed to giving up control.) Also, you will earn much less income per book sold. On the other hand, if the book becomes a major seller due to the publisher's marketing and distribution resources, you will ultimately be better off financially than if you tried to market and sell the book on your own.

Some of the advantages of self-publishing your book are that you have complete artistic and editorial control and you reap all the profits of any sales. The disadvantages are that you have to get the book together, you will have to do your own editing, you will have to initially put up the money for the printing of the book, and, finally, you will have to market and distribute the book yourself.

Most printing outfits can print books. There are also several Internet sites, such as Booksurge, which enable one to print a book. Also, sites such as Amazon assist self-published authors to market their books.

The bottom line, then, is that writing a book legitimatizes you, gives you credibility, helps you become known as an expert, and, if the book becomes popular, can be a source of passive income. A book also attracts clients bearing cash. Over the years, I have had many clients come to me because they read one of my books or simply heard I wrote a book.

> **4.** Speak Out. Like authoring a book, speaking also leads to you being perceived as an expert. You can speak on the relevant, common topics of interest at the school PTO, a church or temple, or community center. When you present you should distribute your speaking outline printed on your stationary, so all the participants will have your contact information. If you speak to a group of 30 participants or so, assuming you do a reasonable job of communicating, you will be likely to glean one or two clients from that presentation—but not necessarily immediately. Remember, if at all possible, be sure to get the e-mail addresses of the participants. A few days after the presentation follow up with an e-mail to all the participants in which you thank them for attending and provide another tidbit of useful information.

Recently, I attended a well-done presentation on sleep disorders as part of the Arizona State Psychological Annual Convention. The presenter was a young psychologist who recently came to the Valley (Phoenix). He collected the e-mail of every willing participant. Several days after the event he sent out an e-mail to everyone on that list (including myself), with all his contact information, thanking me for attending and providing a sheet on basic sleep intervention techniques which were discussed in his presentation. In addition to having a unique niche, with his effective marketing methods I suspect he should be very busy very soon.

If you become serious about professional speaking, you may want to join Toastmasters and/or a speaker's association. You should also audio- and videotape your presentations and have them critiqued. By becoming an effective, professional speaker you will become known as an expert, additional referral sources will want to work with you, and, undoubtedly, more clients with cash will seek you out.

Another great way to meet and secure referral sources is to make contact with the local organizations to which these professionals belong and ask if you can arrange to provide a presentation. I have spoken at luncheons to physicians, attorneys, and chiropractors and have gleaned many additional referral sources. Remember, always get their e-mail addresses.

> **5.** Talk radio. Most cities have one or two prominent talk radio stations. Talk radio is surprisingly popular. Many, many people listen to their favorite radio station or announcer while they work, relax, and certainly while they drive. (Howard Stern makes how many hundreds of millions of dollars?) Whenever I do a radio show I always get feedback from friends, clients, and referral sources (but I'm no Howard Stern).

Now, of course, you cannot contact a station and ask them to put you on the air because you want to market yourself and become known as the local expert. You will not get far with that. You must offer them something of value: You may suggest that you speak about something in the news from a psychological perspective. You could ask to talk about a recent article or book you authored that has general appeal. Radio stations especially like topical subjects, so I have done shows on the following: "Preparing your kindergartener to start school;" "Helping your child to get better grades;" "How to study effectively;" "Signs your adolescent may be using drugs;" "Increasing communication in your marriage;" and on other similar topics. (By the way, these topics, and others like them, would make an excellent article in the local paper or magazine.)

If interested in talk radio, call the station and ask to speak with the producer of the commentator with whom you wish to work. Let the producer know of your proposed topic. The producer may want some information, such as a vita, to ensure you are legitimate. Since these shows have many hours to fill, they are often eager to work with local talent. If you are persistent, it should not be long before you are on the air.

Participating in talk radio can be fun. It is interesting to see how they produce a show. Things are often a bit "loosey-goosey" on these shows, so just relax and go with the flow. Many of these announcers became popular because of their personality, not because they were great interviewers. Again, relax, have fun, and make your points when you can.

If your segment provides for listener call-in, do not provide individual psychotherapy over the airwaves—like Dr. Phil. Instead, speak on general topics such as parenting, marriage, or depression.

If you do a reasonable job, you likely will be asked back. Take the opportunity. (It was such opportunities that led to me being on the Phil Donahue Show more than a decade ago.) After a handful of segments you will be well on your way to becoming known as a local expert. Whenever you do a show be absolutely certain you receive a copy of your segment. You can use that material for future marketing—including adding a piece of it to your website.

It has been my experience that clients who find me because of my speaking, a radio show, an article, one of my books, or through a referral, are much more likely to pay cash. It seems to me that individuals that take the time and effort to seek out an "expert" are often more willing to pay cash. It is a common refrain in the marketing world that "People buy with their hearts and then use their heads to rationalize their decision." By becoming "the expert" the prospective client is much more inclined to seek you out and gladly pay your fee. (Does someone using their MC benefits truly expect to see an "expert"?)

Develop and reinforce your "brand"

The "brand" I am referring to is not the mark the cowboy burns into the side of the steer. Your brand is your image, your professional reputation, what you hope clients, referral sources, and potential referral sources think of you when they hear or see your name. Companies like Volvo, Toyota, IBM, and Southwest Airlines have certain brands—"safety," "reliability," "strong," and "competitive," respectively. What is your professional brand? Here is mine: "Experienced, ethical, solution-oriented, good communicator, and reliable." This is my professional brand and I strive to live up to and reinforce that image whenever I can.

While doing the research for this book, I came upon a classic, famous McGraw-Hill ad:

"I don't know who you are.

I don't know your company.

I don't know your company's product.

I don't know what your company stands for.

I don't know your company's customers.

I don't know your company's record.

I don't know your company's reputation.

Now what is it you wanted to sell me?"

Now this ad, of course, refers to general sales and marketing of products and services, but in many respects it could also apply to mental health marketing. As noted just previously, the marketing starts before you enter the office. If you have developed a brand as an expert and respected professional, you will have eased the way toward garnering more referral sources. In addition, clients are going to be much more willing to work with you if they already know something about you.

Target your referral sources and identify their problems

There are four basic questions in marketing:

1. Who are your customers (in our case—referral sources and clients) for your service?

2. What kinds of problems do these people have?

3. What can you do to address their problems?

4. How can you reach these people?

As noted, a basic rule of marketing is to define your target—or, in our case, your potential referral sources. Do not simply go out of your office, walk across the street to the neighboring medical complex, knock on every door, and drop off your card. You want to identify your referral sources so you can convey to them the right message. T. Harv Eker, a currently popular financial wellness and motivation speaker, says, "An entrepreneur solves problems for others for money." Along those lines, then, the correct message I believe you want to send to your potential referral sources consists of three basic components:

1. You understand the specific problems that particular referral source has.

2. You are an expert (or, at least, proficient) in dealing with those issues.

3. You can construct solutions to those problems.

As noted previously, the importance of speaking in terms of solutions rather than procedures cannot be overstated. Therefore, when you finally get an audience with a potential referral source, you will want to keep the above three points firmly in mind.

In the next chapter I will speak about soliciting those potential referral sources.

Important points to remember in CHAPTER SEVEN:

1. You can transition from a MC practice to a fee-for-service one gradually—you do not have to cancel all your MC contracts at once.

2. You should market to the masses—not just to the "sick"

3. Marketing copy should be concise, simple, behaviorally-oriented, with no psychobabble.

4. Become the "expert" by writing articles, connecting with reporters, writing a book, and speaking out.

5. Develop and reinforce your "brand."

6. Target your referral sources and identify their problems.

Action steps to take from CHAPTER SEVEN:

1. If you desire to move toward a cash-pay practice, rank in order your MC companies from least-favorite to favorite. Determine a date by which you resign from your least-favorite firm.

2. Review your marketing copy to ensure it is simple, action/solution-oriented, and free of psychobabble.

3. Determine a strategy that you will use to become the "expert." Set a date by which you will have written that article or book or arranged a speaking date.

4. Write down in a few words or in a sentence what your "brand" is. Refer to these adjectives or characteristics in your marketing copy and ensure your behavior reinforces your brand.

5. Identify two potential referral sources and their needs and set a date by when you will have made contact with them.

It will never rain roses: when we want to have more roses we must plant more trees.

George Eliot

CHAPTER EIGHT

SOLICITING PHYSICIANS AND OTHER PROFESSIONALS

Soliciting physicians

Physicians are likely to be an important referral source for just about any mental health practice—and most especially for a cash-pay practice. So how do you get to meet doctors?

First, I recommend that you read the local newspaper, and especially the smaller local paper that targets the particular part of the city in which you practice. I suggest you always be on the lookout for ads in which medical groups announce the addition of a new physician to their group and, most especially, other ads in which a new medical practice is being opened. If a new medical practitioner is coming to your area, why not be the first mental health provider to meet with him and welcome him? This new physician is probably quite interested in developing a referral network, so it would make good sense to meet with that doctor and try to be at the top of his list for psychological referrals.

If you are seeking cash-pay clients, it probably makes the most sense to solicit physicians that see patients that can more readily afford fee-for-service. Nevertheless, my colleague with the strictly cash-pay practice has several physicians who are located in central Phoenix and still refer him a steady stream of cash-pay patients.

If I have targeted a particular physician, usually I have my secretary call that office and indicate that Dr. Waldman would like to take just five minutes of their time to introduce himself and his services, and schedule an appointment. My secretary will also note that Dr. Waldman is open to having lunch or breakfast with the doctor, as well. By scheduling an appointment, I rarely get turned down.

On occasion I will just drop in at an office. Recently, for example, I went to my primary care physician for my annual physical. Next door, in the adjoining office, I noticed that a neurologist had just moved in. So, since I was in the neighborhood, I stopped in and managed to have a nice chat with the young physician.

MDs and their offices are accustomed to having people stopping in, as pharmacy representatives do so all the time. Ever wonder why 95 percent of pharmacy representatives are young, attractive women? That is because most of the male docs would be more willing to see them. Nevertheless, while I am certainly not young, or attractive, for that matter, I attempt to drop in and visit briefly with a physician once in awhile.

Most physicians start their day at 9:00 a.m., break for lunch at noon, resume seeing patients at 1:30 p.m., and end their day at about 5:00 p.m. If I choose to "drop in" on a physician, these are the times (9:00, noon, 1:30, and 5:00) that are least obtrusive to the physician's practice and may facilitate you getting in faster to visit with the doctor.

When I get an audience with a physician I first promise to take no more than five minutes of their time. I thank them for taking the time to speak for me. I ask them the typical kinds of problems their patients bring to them. I listen to them and then, when appropriate, indicate that I am familiar and comfortable working with these issues. I then mention the observable, measurable goals that I strive to attain with such patients. Importantly, I also will spend a minute talking about my concerns with MC regarding professional control and confidentiality and explain why I prefer to see cash-paying clients. Most physicians relate to what I am saying and many of them have responded to me by saying they wish they could practice that way, too. I again thank them for their time. I always ask them if I can have their e-mail address and if it would be acceptable for me, on occasion, to send them material. I rarely, if ever, have that request denied.

I always bring something to leave with an office I visit. In addition to my business card, of course, I will leave a copy of a recent newsletter, an article I wrote, if it is relevant, or a copy of one of my books. Also, I never forget to "schmooze" with the front office person and most especially with the office manager. In many offices the physician recommends the mental health referral but the person at the front desk or the office manager is often the particular individual who gives the referral to the patient. If the front office person and/or the office manager know you, that referral will be more enthusiastic. I love it when a referred patient comes to me and says that the office manager told her that that their office "sends all their patients to Dr. Waldman. He's really nice. He wrote a book! Everybody we've sent to him has been very happy."

Communicate and follow-up

Within the week of meeting with physicians or potential referral sources I send a hand-written note thanking them for their time. I also add them to my e-mail list and send them my monthly newsletter.

If and when I do receive clients from physicians or other professionals, I ask them if they are okay with me letting the referring professional know that they have followed through with the referral and made and kept their first appointment. Most clients not only authorize me to contact their referring physician or professional, they want me to do so and are glad that I suggested it. (I note that authorization in the file, of course.)

When I see a newly-referred client I now have an opportunity to write that physician or professional and thank him for the referral. I very briefly and generally note the patient's or client's concerns, what I intend to do, and indicate that I will re-contact them when the treatment episode is complete. In this manner, I am reinforcing that physician or professional for the referral, effectively communicating with them regarding a mutual client, and will have gotten my name, on paper, again, in front of them at least twice.

Physicians really like it when their medical records reflect a referral, the receipt of the referral, and a final note upon completion or termination of the treatment. I have had many physicians tell me that the number one thing they like about me is that I communicate with them. Several physicians have complained to me that when they make a referral to some other mental health provider, they have no idea if the client ever made it there, if their patient was ever seen, whether the treatment was successful or not, or if the patient terminated the treatment prematurely. Physicians are most likely going to continue to refer to a mental health provider who effectively communicates with them.

A critical component of effective marketing is repetition. In marketing parlance, this is referred to as "dripping." Think about the last time you purchased something substantial—such as a car, appliance, an electronic component, or a nice bicycle, for example. . You probably did not walk into the store and buy the first item you saw. It is more likely you did some research and relied heavily on name recognition. Marketing research clearly shows that people often must have frequent exposures to a product or an ad before they will act on it. (That is why we keep seeing all those recurring ads on TV.) Therefore, the more times you can get your name in front of a referral source or potential referral source, the more likely that referral source will think of you and send you clients.

Schultz and Doerr, in their book *Professional Services Marketing*, 2009, noted the following marketing copy, written by a Thomas Smith, in 1885!!

The first time people look at a given ad, they don't even see it.
The second time, they don't notice it.
The third time, they are aware that it is there.
The fourth time, they have a fleeting sense that they've seen it somewhere before
The fifth time, they actually read the ad.
The sixth time, they thumb their nose at it.
The seventh time, they start to get a little irritated with it.

The eighth time, they start to think, "Here's that confounded ad again."

The ninth time, they start to wonder that they may be missing out on something.

The tenth time, they ask their friends and neighbors if they've tried it.

The eleventh time, they wonder how this company is paying for all those ads.

The twelfth time, they start to think that it must be a good product.

The thirteenth time, they start to feel the product has value.

The fourteenth time, they start to remember wanting a product exactly like this for a long time.

The fifteenth time, they start to yearn for it because they can't afford to buy it.

The sixteenth time, they accept the fact that they will buy it sometime in the future.

The seventeenth time, they make a note to buy the product.

The eighteenth time, they curse their poverty for not allowing them to buy this terrific product.

The nineteenth time, they count their money very carefully.

The twentieth time prospects see the ad, they buy what it is offering.

Apparently, things have not changed much in the marketing and sales arena in 125 years! Of course, I am not suggesting that you have to visit with prospective referral sources 20 times before they will begin referring to you, but clearly it will take more than one brief contact to establish a referral connection.

There have been times when I met with a potential referral source and had, I thought, a nice interaction, but I never heard from that source again. On the other hand, I have had rushed chats with physicians that resulted in excellent referral sources. You never really know what the future will bring, so you keep trying.

Many mental health professionals have a nice visit with a potential referral source, write a nice thank you note, and then assume the referrals will stream in. If they do not hear from that referral source after a time, they will have no further contact with him or her. As already noted, you cannot expect that one brief visit will establish a long-term referral pattern. It will probably take more than that—such as an additional personal contact, a newsletter, a copy of an article, or a good word from an associate.

It is important to follow up even with established referral sources because things can always change. What if a new mental health professional moves into the same professional complex as your referral source, for example? Years ago, in the late 1980's, I had a pediatric group that referred exclusively to me. I received one to three referrals a week from that group and they were, by far, my most important referral source at that time. After working successfully with them for several years I received an announcement inviting me to come to a luncheon welcoming a new pediatrician to their group. I RSVP'd, of course, as I would not want to pass up the opportunity to interact with the doctors and the staff—not to mention meet the new physician and "bring him or her into the fold."

During the luncheon I had the chance to meet and chat with the new, young physician. After a bit he noted that his wife had not joined him yet from Boston because she was completing her degree. When I inquired what field her degree was in, he answered, "She is just about done with her Ph.D. and internship in clinical child psychology from Harvard." Within six months this young Ph.D. had joined her husband in Phoenix, opened her practice, and my referrals from that group immediately slowed to a trickle. The moral of the story is, of course, "Never stop marketing!"

When I develop an established referral source, a medical group for example, and have a chance to speak with them I often ask if they might have a colleague that they think could also benefit from my services. With this "piggy-back" system, I am often able to secure another opportunity to meet with another potential referral source. Often, I ask my established referral source if he or his office staff would make an introductory call for me to the other professional announcing that I will be calling on him or her; I have never had that request denied.

Importantly, when one of my clients who was not referred to me by a particular professional asks for a referral, I regularly will attempt to send that person to one of my referral sources, if I believe the referral is appropriate, of course. Unquestionably, referring clients back to your referral sources is a highly potent way of maintaining an effective referral network. Recently, for example, I met and had breakfast with a new, young child psychiatrist, who works exclusively on a cash basis, who sent me a case shortly after we met. There was little doubt in my mind that the next client who asks me about a child psychiatrist in that vicinity will be given her name.

Typical problems physicians face

Since I do a lot of work with children, let us first consider the problems pediatricians are confronted with on a daily basis: Parents complain their children misbehave, continue to wet their bed, have poor eating or sleeping pattern, do not seem to learn effectively, are socially withdrawn or inept, are anxious, or might potentially have attention deficit disorder. To effectively market yourself to a pediatrician, then, you should be able to indicate that you are familiar with such issues and are capable of developing solutions for such concerns.

Consider some of the other basic issues faced by the following medical professionals:

Family practice physician:

Depression, anxiety, marital problems, stress, parenting issues, weight control, alcohol and/or tobacco addictions.

Internal medicine physician:

There is much overlap with the family physician but, in addition, internists deal with chronic medical conditions, like diabetes, chronic fatigue syndrome, and fibromyalgia.

OBG:

Sexual issues, marital problems, depression.

Neurologist:

Issues related to brain damage, dementia, psychological evaluations and neuropsychological evaluations for brain dysfunction, learning disabilities, and attention deficit disorder.

Psychiatrist:

Psychological evaluations for differential diagnosis and psychotherapy for patients on psychotropic medication.

Of course, there are other medical specialties which have their own particular patient problems that a mental health professional can address.

Soliciting attorneys

What I have just discussed with respect to physicians—targeting, identifying the problems, emphasizing the solutions, communicating after the meeting, getting e-mail addresses, and branding—all applies to attorneys, as well. I especially like working with attorneys because of the following:

1. Since legal work is not health-related, insurance is not involved. (I have had many cases where clients attempt to use their insurance for court-ordered evaluations and even for family studies. I regularly tell these clients that their concern is a legal one, not a health issue—no one is "sick." Therefore, their health insurance does not apply. Can you imagine submitting a bill to MC for multiple sessions with every member of a family all within a 45-day period?!)

2. It is perfectly ethical to charge a higher "legal" rate for this type of work, because forensic work is held to a much higher level of scrutiny—as attorneys and judges review it and there may well be depositions and/or expert testimony required. If the average rate for a family law attorney in Phoenix is presently about $325.00 per hour, I think it is more than appropriate that a psychologist charge at least about two-thirds of that for forensic psychological work.

It is appropriate and acceptable when solicited for a deposition or subpoenaed to testify, to charge for "preparation time" and "travel time"—to and from the office. You should also charge for the cost of canceling clients, if you are called to a deposition or a court hearing at the last minute. A higher fee should be charged for actual deposition time and for testifying in court. I always get the money well ahead of time. For a typical four-hour deposition, I can earn upwards of $1,500.00. (Remember, the two attorneys are each earning double that.) There is likely to be some stress involved with this work, but on the other hand, I would have to see 30 MC clients to earn about the same fee. Now that's real stress!

Many mental health professionals fear and avoid the legal arena. Most mental health providers are not comfortable being scrutinized and having their work challenged. Recently, a colleague asked me why I am not intimidated by attorneys. I replied, "Since my older son, Josh, is an attorney, I've diapered one."

3. While forensic work can be stressful but remunerative, it is also professionally interesting and challenging. Also, frankly, I glean more professional respect and satisfaction doing this work.

Family law attorneys

Family law or domestic relations attorneys can be a rich source of referrals. As noted previously, essentially any referral from an attorney will be expected to be on a cash-pay basis. Family law attorneys have the following needs:

> **1.** On occasion they require a mental health professional to conduct a comprehensive family study (custody evaluation) to assess the family and possibly make recommendations to the Court with respect to the best interests of the children concerning parental custody and access.

I especially like these referrals because they pay quite well. The fee for a custody evaluation can run anywhere from four thousand to 10 thousand dollars. Moreover, a family study is quite professionally challenging, as it involves clinical interviewing, dealing with adults and children, psychometrics, effective report writing, and interacting with other mental health providers, attorneys, and the Court.

> **2.** Family law attorneys have many clients who are going through possibly one of the most stressful periods of their lives, most especially if the divorce is being contested and/or a custody dispute is involved. Many individuals going through divorce frequently contact their divorce attorney seeking guidance, reassurance, and just a sensitive ear. These contacts can be expensive and sometimes bothersome to the attorney, as the attorney is not a trained therapist. A mental health professional can

provide a great service to the attorney by working with these clients as they go through this very difficult time in their lives. If the psychotherapist is familiar with the local divorce procedures, that also would be quite useful.

3. Family law attorneys regularly hear from clients that their children are having a difficult time adjusting to the separation and divorce. Once again, a mental health professional could provide a valuable service in this arena.

4. Family law attorneys often need a mental health professional who can provide co-parenting counseling. This is a situation where the parents are about to be divorced or are recently divorced and need help learning how to deal with the children effectively and appropriately. Sometimes this process is Court-ordered.

5. Family law attorneys occasionally need a mental health professional to provide "therapeutic reintegration" services. This is the situation where, for one reason or another, a parent has been absent or distant from a child's life or alienated from the child, and that parent wants to re-connect with the child. Often, this process is also Court-ordered.

6. Family law attorneys occasionally have a need to have their client or the opposing counsel's client evaluated. This situation typically occurs when one parent alleges that the other parent is not psychologically fit to see the children or visit with the children in an unsupervised manner and the attorney wants an assessment of this parent. Once more, these evaluations frequently are Court-ordered.

7. Finally, family law attorneys often have a need to have a mental health professional appointed as a Parenting Coordinator (PC) or Family Court Advisor (FCA). In the past few years several states have adopted this concept. A PC or FCA is usually appointed by the Court to help divorced couples resolve some of their post-divorce issues without going back to Court and adding to the Court's backlog or re-contacting their respective attorneys and spending more money. I usually have two to five PC sessions per week and charge about $250 for each of these sessions. While at first glance this may seem expensive, but given that the parties could each spend $350 dollars for that per hour with their respective attorney, the PC process saves parents a significant amount of money. Though these sessions can be stressful, I believe PC work can truly help families during a difficult period in their lives.

If you are interested in doing family law work—which I encourage you to consider—you could make contact with the local family law judges, as they often order that mental health professionals become involved in their cases. You could also write to them, noting your clinical experience and desire to work in the field of domestic relations, and set an appointment to meet with a judge. If the PC/FCA concept has not yet come to your locale, you might consider researching the idea and work toward bringing it to your area. If you are responsible for bringing this process to your area, you'll likely be the mental health professional who will get most of the referrals—at least for an initial period of time. You might also be asked to train others in this procedure.

Defense attorneys

Defense attorneys are also a good source of referrals:

1. Defense attorneys occasionally want their clients to get into treatment. Like family law attorneys, defense attorneys are not trained nor have the time to counsel their clients. In addition, if the clients can demonstrate that they have engaged in treatment, chances are their sentence might be reduced. Also, family members of the perpetrators, or the victims, for that matter, may be in need of treatment, as well.

Defense attorneys occasionally want their client to undergo an evaluation to help with the defense case. Recently, for example, I was asked by a defense attorney to examine a young man who was facing some substantial prison time, as he was apprehended for shoplifting for the third or fourth time. My assessment indicated this individual had undiagnosed and untreated ADHD, which, I believe, played a significant role in his illegal behavior. The judge accepted my report and sentenced the young man to probation and Court-order treatment, instead of a few years in prison—which probably would have done little, ultimately, for the individual, and our society.

Personal injury (PI) attorneys

PI attorneys are excellent sources of referrals, too. PI attorneys represent individuals who have been injured due to motor vehicle accidents (MVAs), dog bites, job accidents, and/or other acts of negligence. A significant part of my forensic practice is to evaluate the emotional state of the victim, document the psychological component of the case, if any, and treat the victim—usually often for PTSD. I have also been involved with PI cases involving medical malpractice and wrongful death, by evaluating and treating the loved ones of the victim. Along these lines, I'm currently planning on soliciting employment attorneys to work with them regarding cases of improper termination.

For more information on working with other attorneys, such as immigration or estate planning attorneys, please check my website, www.MentalHealthMarketingAcademy.com.

Chiropractors

Many people use their chiropractor essentially as their family doctor. Thus, like the family doctor, chiropractors are good referral sources. Moreover, most victims of MVAs see chiropractors for their back and neck pain. Therefore, chiropractors are also excellent referral sources for PI cases. My experience with chiropractors is that they are generally quite open and appreciative of mental health providers calling on them because, as a rule, physicians often have little to do with chiropractors. Doctors of Chiropractic (DCs) seem to relate well with mental health providers because both groups are holistic in their approach and are less steeped in the medical model.

Dentists

Dentists tend to see people when they are in pain and are not at their best. Therefore, dentists are a fair source of referrals. Pediadontists, or pediatric dentists, on the other hand, can be a much richer source of referrals.

School psychologists and school counselors

School psychologists and school counselors daily see children and teens that can use the services of a private mental health provider. Thus, they can be a decent source of referrals. While the school professionals certainly have access to a large number of potential clients, the major problem is that few of these referrals will follow up and fewer will pay cash for private service. As an ex-school psychologist of years ago, I understand school psychologists and school counselors generally come to the parent but, in the private sector, the parents come to the provider. Therefore, only a small number of parents will follow up on a referral and, since the parent is coming from the public sector and getting free service, only a few parents will choose to pay cash for treatment. School psychologists and school counselors, thus, can be a better source for MC referrals.

Clergy

You might be surprised at the number of people who share their personal problems with their priest, minister, deacon, or rabbi. The clergy, then, are potentially good referral sources. Often, for example, the church, mosque, or synagogue will pay the treatment bill. You can enter this arena of working with clergy initially by speaking to your own religious leader.

Other mental health providers

If you have a particular skill or practice in a unique area, you should let other mental health providers know of this. For example, if you do biofeedback, EMDR, psychological testing, or work with sleep disorders, sexual abuse of children, cancer survivors, or do forensic work, you could easily receive referrals from fellow mental health providers who do not choose to do this type of work. These mental health providers/referral sources, of course, will have to know you exist, respect you professionally, and trust that you will not "steal" their patient, if they refer a client to you for a consultation.

HR Directors

If you manage to make contact with a business, which will be discussed in the next chapter, that HR department may well become a great source of cash-pay referrals. Years ago, I made a connection with the HR VP of a local bank. For several years, he referred many high-level executives and their family members to me—and the HR Department paid the full bill. Also, if any bank was the victim of a hold-up or attempted hold-up, every employee at that branch was told to see me—for free—and the full fee was paid by HR.

(Hopefully, this discussion gives you some new marketing target ideas.)

Important points to remember in CHAPTER EIGHT:

1. Check the newspaper for announcements of the opening of new medical practices—and be one of the first mental health providers to greet them.

2. Make appointments to visit with MDs. If you choose to just drop by, do so at 9am, noon, 1:30pm, or 5pm.

3. Have the MD speak about the problems his/her patients have and note that you can provide solutions to them.

4. If you are seeking cash-pay clients, speak to the MD about your concerns with MC.

5. Always leave something and send a thank-you note.

6. If you get an MD referral, acknowledge it.

7. If you develop a referral relationship with an MD (or any other professional, for that matter) ask them if they could refer you to a colleague who could also use your services.

8. Attorneys are excellent referral sources for clinical as well as legal cases.

9. Chiropractors, dentists, school psychologists and counselors, clergy persons, other mental health providers, and HR directors, are all good referral sources.

Action steps to take from CHAPTER EIGHT:

1. Vow to contact at least two MDs and two attorneys per month for the next 12 months.

2. Vow to contact at least one non-traditional referral source each month—chiropractor, dentist, clergy person, school psychologist, for example.

3. Write your thank-you notes and acknowledgments of referrals.

Once in motion, a pattern tends to stay in motion.

J. G. Gallimore

People say to me, You were a roaring success. How did you do it? I go back to what my parents taught me. Apply yourself. Get all the education you can, but then, by God, do something. Don't just stand there, make something happen.

Lee Iacocca

CHAPTER NINE

NON-TRADITIONAL WAYS TO EARN INCOME AS A MENTAL HEALTH PROVIDER

The following are a number of non-traditional methods of earning income as a mental health provider:

Groups

Running groups out of your office can be an interesting, challenging, and lucrative way to produce income. All sorts of groups are possible, for example: Parenting, Marital, Men's, Women's, Socialization for Children or Teens, Adult Children of Alcoholics, Survivors of Sexual Abuse, Dealing with Chronic Illness, Bipolar Disorder, Depression, OCD, Smoking Cessation, and Weight Loss.

Getting a group together and up and running is probably the most difficult part of doing group work. The groups can be time-limited or on-going, depending on your preference. Once you have started several groups, the word will get out and forming new groups or getting new group members, will be easier. A good resource for group members is other mental health providers, as most mental health providers do not choose to do group work.

You can run 8 to 12 persons (or more?) in a group. You could easily charge $40.00 to $60.00 each for a group session. (Interestingly, MC pays reasonably for group treatment—about $40.00 to $50.00 per session.) If you have 10 persons, say, in your group each paying, say, $50.00 per session, you can earn a rather nice fee for the 90-minute group. If you were to run three 10-person groups per week, your monthly income would be boosted by about $6,000.00. That should help with the bottom line. I know of a counselor in the Valley who runs two to three groups per day, three to four days per week and has developed a lucrative cash practice.

Coaching

Coaching currently is in its infancy as a profession but it is growing all the time. You can take coursework or attend seminars and become certified as a coach but presently there is no accepted entity that credentials coaches. Many persons doing coaching today are not certified, do not have a graduate degree, and some do not even have a Bachelor's degree. Clearly, with some training, a licensed mental health provider could easily make the transition to coaching.

Coaching does not concern itself with mental illness. Instead, coaching assists people to achieve their goals—"helps them become all they can be." Most of the coaching being done today, I believe, is associated with business executives, assisting them to become more efficient managers and leaders. There are, however, many other arenas in which coaching is being done: Helping persons laid off find appropriate jobs; helping mothers re-enter the work world; helping high school graduates transition successfully into college; helping young mothers and fathers become more effective parents; helping and encouraging entrepreneurs to stay with their projects and become successful; and weight loss. Almost any area outside the arena of mental illness could become a reasonable coaching target.

From a practice-development perspective, coaching could be considered or should be considered because it is a strictly cash-pay enterprise. Since mental health concerns are not involved, at least in theory, insurance reimbursement does not apply. In addition, some coaching today is done remotely—by phone, videoconferencing, or even by instant messaging. Under these circumstances, then, your client base for coaching is no longer just the immediate vicinity of your office, but, essentially, it is worldwide. If you intend to engage in remote coaching, you will have to become quite familiar with Internet marketing—(as will be discussed in the next and final chapter). At any rate, coaching could be a nice adjunct to your practice.

Professional speaking

Earlier, I spoke about public speaking as a means to become known as an expert. Speaking can also be a way to earn additional income—sometimes substantial additional income. From my perspective, instead of speaking with one person for one hour for $100.00 in a session, I would prefer to speak in front of 100 persons for a few hours, with each person paying me $25.00. Clearly, successful speaking affords the opportunity to earn considerably more income than seeing individual patients in the office.

T. Harv Eker, the motivational speaker I referred to previously, teaches that with regard to speaking, "The money is in the back end." For example, I recently was asked to give a 90-minute evening talk for the parents of a large, successful, active private school. The deal I made with the principal was that my fee was $250.00 for the seminar, but if 40 or more parents were in attendance, I would drop the fee to $100.00. (In this fashion the school is motivated to really encourage parents to attend.) In fact, nearly 50 parents came.

In the back of the room my wife, Nan, sat a table on which all of my books, relaxation CD, and CDs of my other presentations, were available for sale. By the end of the evening I had sold nearly $1,000.00 worth of products, of which about 90% was pure profit. The $900.00 profit, all from "the back end," was a nice ROI (return on my investment)—on my 90 minutes of time. By the way, I donated the $100.00 "front end" fee back to the school to ensure that I can do "a return engagement" at that school in the near future. Moreover, since I was asked for my business card a dozen or so times, I am anticipating a number of (cash-paying) clients, as well.

What if you do not have any books or CDs to sell? Produce them! As I noted earlier, books and CDs develop credibility and afford passive income. However, if you cannot produce a book or a CD, at least in the near future, you can always sell additional speaking. Let me suggest the following:

You contact your church, mosque, or temple, or child's parent-teacher organization, or your health club, or your community center and propose to present an introductory 90-minute seminar on....whatever (parenting, couples communication, stress management, mindfulness). You indicate you will charge a nominal fee, like $20 to $25 per person, and you will remit 20% of the proceeds to the organization for the use of their room and for their promotion of the event by way of their newsletter and bulletins posted on the wall. The organization will most likely be happy to sponsor the event since it costs them nothing to promote it in the newsletter and it provides the opportunity for the organization to put some additional funds in their coffers and do something a little bit different.

When you present the initial introductory seminar, try to have something else to sell to increase profits—perhaps a manuscript (if the book is incomplete) or an article of yours. Upon completion of the introductory seminar, you then offer a follow-up, more intensive, three- or four-evening program (three or four consecutive Tuesday evenings, for example) for a fee of about $125.00 to $175.00 per person or 1.5 times that amount per couple, if appropriate (such as parenting or couples' communication). Hopefully, you will attract about a quarter of the initial group who will sign up for the more intense program. Of course, the sponsoring organization gets its 20% of the follow-up program, as well.

If you have, say, 12 persons (hopefully more) paying you about $150.00 each for three to four evenings (minus the 20% commission) you are earning several hundred dollars per evening, which, again, certainly beats MC pricing—and the speaking time is probably outside of regular office hours, anyhow. In addition, your name in the newsletter is free advertising (whether someone comes or not), and several clients are also likely to come out of the event as well. The beauty of this approach is that you do not have to concern yourself with finding a room or marketing the event, as the organization does all of that for you. If the program is a success—and why wouldn't it be?—you can offer additional ones.

As you develop your speaking skills and reputation, you can expand your speaking opportunities. Recently I attended a local one-day seminar on Solution-Focused Marital Therapy. The fee was a nominal $99.00 but I counted over 80 heads in the audience. My quick figuring was the total take, minus the expenses (mailings, hotel conference room, coffee service, and the commission paid to the sponsoring professional organization), left this professional with approximately $6-$7,000.00 for his efforts. That is not a bad day's work!

Several years ago I attended a local, day-long seminar conducted by Elbert Ellis. The event was sponsored by a local therapist. The fee, I seem to recall, was about $200.00. There were well over 100 persons in attendance. I thought that professional used an innovative way to make a few bucks—and earn CE units in the process.

I have also checked into some of those CE outfits that regularly send mental health providers those brochures. If you have a topic that the company thinks will sell, they might be willing to put you in their "stable" of speakers. The company does all the promotion, by way of mailings, and pays all your expenses. Your fee is essentially based on the number of paid attendees. You can make as little as $400.00 per day or up to $2,000.00 per day, if one hundred persons sign up. For some providers, including myself, to take a day or so out of the office to make a few hundred dollars does not make much economic sense. On the other hand, if you like to travel, have something additional to sell, and can schedule your clients around your travel time, you might want to contact one of these companies. By the way, some of these companies also provide continuing education to physicians and attorneys, so if you have something to offer those groups, you could make yourself even more attractive. (How about: "Preparing Your Client for a Custody Evaluation" or "Recognizing and Managing PTSD in the PI Client," or "Basic CBT for the Treatment of Depression for the Family Physician")

Consulting to private and/or charter schools

Private or charter schools have the need for the services of a school psychologist, counselor, or behavioral interventionist, but often do not need nor can afford one on a full-time basis. Therefore, they frequently are in the market to contract with such a professional for perhaps a day per week. In this manner you can infuse some cash into your practice. Also, since the school day ends usually by 3 p.m. or so you can return to the office and see a few clients that evening, if you choose.

Consulting to business and industry

Consulting to business is an excellent way to earn substantial additional income. Probably the best way to get in the door with larger local employers is to offer to do a free seminar. (Remember, the money is in the "back end.") The common seminar topics could be on such topics as effective communication, stress management, or burn-out. Most of the time, these types of presentations are arranged through the HR department.

If the first presentation goes well, you probably will be asked to do another—and hopefully others. Your objective is to become recognized as an expert and as a valuable resource.

Once this happens you may be asked to consult with supervisors and administrators on areas of leadership, employee motivation, downsizing, managing conflict, and other issues—and you will be paid well to do so. You can also become a special part of the company's employee assistance program (EAP) and clinically see managers, and higher level staff, as needed. If the company really likes your work, they may send you to other company sites around the country. As you become known as an "industrial consultant," it will be easier to land other consulting opportunities.

Social Security

The Social Security Administration hires or contracts with a very large number of psychologists. Most of these professionals provide "consultative evaluations" (CEs) in their offices (usually) to individuals who are applying for Social Security but have no current or appropriate treating sources (TSs) that can provide acceptable medical information. In Phoenix there are several psychologists who do the majority of CEs and have developed a lucrative practice in the process. Some psychologists do these evaluations on a part-time basis to fill in difficult-to-book early morning hours. I assume nearly every major city has a Social Security office. Contact the office in your area if you are interested in this type of consultative work.

Sports psychology

A few years ago a couple brought their adolescent daughter to me. She was number one on her high school tennis team but was losing most of her close matches. Her parents believed that psychological reasons were behind these losses and asked me if I could help. Having played a number of sports in my time, including tennis, I said I believed I could be of some assistance.

Using basic cognitive techniques, in addition to some imagery and relaxation methods, I helped this teen recognize and conquer the "stinking thinking" she was doing during a match—especially in a competitive one. In a short time my client began to perform at the level commensurate with her physical talent. She won the regional championship and reportedly lost a hard-fought match in the state finals. She also secured a college tennis scholarship.

Word of my success with this case spread and soon I was seeing several other players. I find it quite enjoyable working with healthy, motivated athletes. Of course, since no one is "sick," insurance is never an issue and this process is strictly one of fee-for-service. If you know or care about anything involving athletics, sports psychology could be an enjoyable and financially rewarding area to explore. If you are truly interested in this field, do some reading, take some workshops, and investigate becoming competent and certified in this arena of opportunity.

Jury selection

In civil cases where a significant amount of money is involved or in a major criminal case (I'm thinking OJ), a jury consultant is often involved. The research is, frankly, sketchy on the actual efficacy of this work, but some attorneys like to cover all their bases and use such consultants.

This work sounds interesting and most likely pays very well. It seems to me that a forensically-sensitive mental health professional could readily make the transition to jury consultant.

I am unaware of any specific training programs for this field, but there are books you can read (see my biography) and occasionally workshops you can attend. To get into this field I imagine you would first contact someone who is already doing this work and arrange some kind of mentoring.

Taking advantage of the crisis in Acute Care

As I noted earlier, a crisis has existed for the past decade in the area of acute mental health care—and I do not see things getting any better in the near future. The problem, simply put, is that MC will only pay for acute care for crisis stabilization. The result is that individuals who need more extensive treatment are forced to go without it or seek it at some very expensive private facility in a far away location. The last decent such facility was pushed out of Phoenix by MC about a decade ago.

For example, in my hometown of Phoenix, a city fast approaching a population of two million, the nearest continued care facilities are either 50 miles northwest—in Wickenburg—or a hundred miles south—in Tucson. Often, these facilities require a commitment of a several-weeks stay. Since they are "the only game in town" there usually is a waiting list for patients who are clamoring to come in and spend $50,000 for their treatment.

In addition to these programs being quite expensive, the patient is logistically cut off from their friends and loved ones (though some of the programs have "family week"), there may be no step-down programs (such as day treatment or intensive outpatient—IOP) and, very importantly, the opportunities for effective aftercare are obviously limited. Based on some limited research, it appears this situation exists not only in Arizona but in many large cities across the country.

If I were 10 years younger, this would be my plan: I would form a partnership with several other mental health providers, including a few psychiatrists who are willing to work cooperatively with psychologists and therapists. I would try to raise the necessary capital among ourselves, or find some investors. I would look to probably lease a facility and most likely would have to so some remodeling. Of course, we would have to obtain the necessary licenses and approvals, but since we would not be using insurance and will not classify ourselves as a "hospital," we would avoid a substantial amount of red tape.

Programmatically, we would have to decide what patient groups we would serve—adults, adult drug and alcohol, adolescents, adolescent drug and alcohol, children, and/or adolescent residential treatment center (RTC). (There is a crying need for good adolescent RTCs.) The treatment program would, in my view, be tailored to the patient rather than have the patient fit into a fixed program. Every patient does not require a 30-to-45-day stay. The program would include a comprehensive workup of the patient within the first 48 hours—history and physical (H&P), psychiatric exam, and a comprehensive psychological evaluation. Patients would attend three to four groups per day and see their psychiatrist and therapist daily. Medications would be provided as needed. Family therapy would be provided at least once per week—or more if clinically indicated. Patients would be "stepped-down" in intensiveness in treatment, depending on their progress—inpatient, to day treatment, to IOP, to twice-weekly outpatient (OP) therapy, to once-weekly OP therapy, to once per month OP therapy, and so on. There would also be on-going aftercare groups for patients and their families. In this manner, patients receive the specific treatment they require and, importantly, their families are inextricably involved with the treatment. The cost for the treatment is strictly fee-for-service.

Of course, this type of treatment is expensive, relative to the "treatment"—using the term very loosely—one may receive through MC. However, there are hundreds, probably thousands, of individuals who need intensive mental health treatment but will get no real help from 72 hours in a MC-directed psychiatric facility but, unfortunately, cannot afford a $50,000 one-month or more stay in a private, out-of town facility. With my proposed tailor-made, step-down program, an episode of treatment may cost about $15,000. For individuals who truly need intensive services, this kind of fee is manageable.

My vision is that with the above model, you will be able to provide a great service to needy patients and to your community—and you will make a bucketful of money at the same time. What could be better?! Moreover, once you perfect the model, you can replicate it elsewhere. You could then franchise the concept and/or sell it and you, your partners, and your investors could all retire early.

There is an old saying in business that with every crisis some smart people figure out a way to take advantage of the situation. This crisis in acute care has gone on for more than a decade and I am surprised no one has yet taken advantage of it. If you want to discuss this concept more fully with me, contact me at:

MentalHealthMarketingAcademy.com or
LarryWaldmanPhD@cox.net

Important points to remember in CHAPTER NINE:

1. There are numerous other ways for a mental health provider to earn income—good income—other than sitting across a client in a therapy office. Some opportunities to consider are to: run groups; become a coach; professionally speak and sell products; consult to private or charter schools; consult to business and industry; consult to Social Security; do sports psychology; become a jury consultant; and start your own psychiatric/psychological care facility.

Action steps to take from CHAPTER NINE:

1. Vow to consider at least one of the just-noted alternative methods of earning income—or derive one of your own—and pursue it until it becomes an important part of your practice. Set dates by which certain steps will have been taken.

Dreaming is wonderful, goal setting is crucial, but action is supreme. To make something great happen you must get busy and make it happen. Take that action step today that will put you on your path to achievement.

Greg Werner

CHAPTER TEN

MARKETING YOUR PRACTICE ONLINE

Newsletters

The use of a newsletter, of course, is nothing new. However, the use of an online newsletter is relatively new and is an innovative concept. As I have already noted, electronically sending a monthly newsletter by e-mail to current and past clients/patients and to current and prospective referral sources is an excellent way to stay connected with these important people. In your newsletter you can make any kind of an announcement you would like—such as a recent article, a new book, up-coming workshop, or new training you have received. For more information on creating a newsletter, please consult MentalHealthMarketingAcademy.com.

Develop a website

There simply is no question about it that people today are increasingly getting all their information from the Internet. Who uses the Yellow Pages today? The prevailing decline of the newspaper across this country is simply due to the fact that most people, especially those under 40, prefer to read the news off a computer screen. Therefore, for mental health providers to effectively market themselves today, they <u>must</u> have a website.

As I previously noted, only 32% of Arizona psychologists I surveyed in the spring of 2009 had their own website. Unfortunately, only a small percent of them realized any or many clients from their site. Most people, including most mental health providers, believe that all you have to do is to slap some website up on the net and the referrals will roll on in. As my survey has shown, this clearly is not the case.

For a website to be effective it not only has to be esthetically pleasing, it must also be technically designed so it will bring users to it. Most prospective clients are not likely to first directly go to your name or site on the net because they probably will not know you. Most prospective clients will first go to a search engine, like Google or Yahoo, and then check out the top listings that are displayed for psychologists, counselors and therapists.

Internet researchers have found that if your site does not come up on the first page, only a very few users will click to the subsequent pages and ever find you. For that matter if your site is not at or near the top of the first page, your site will get relatively few "hits." The reason for this seems to be that people are lazy and people believe that the top listings are the better or more important ones.

Therefore, regardless how attractive or innovative your site may be, unless it comes up high on most search engine pages, it will not be an effective client-gathering tool. To get a site to come up high or highest on the page requires that it be designed according to notions of "search engine optimization" (SEO). Frankly, this technical concept is beyond my understanding, but what it basically means is that you must hire a professional to design a truly effective, client-gathering website.

In November 2009 my partner and technical guru in the Mental Health Marketing Academy did some basic research. He found that there are, on average, 74 "hits" per day on the search for "Phoenix therapist" or "Phoenix psychologist." The number one site on both these searches (that was before my new site was launched) garners 42% of that "traffic." In other words, this number one listing is receiving about 350 "hits" per month.

Now obviously not all those "hits" are going to result in actual clients. Some of those "hits" are simply "shoppers." Yet even if 5 or 10% of those "hits" become clients, that practice will clearly have a nice stream of incoming referrals. (Also, since those "shoppers" are doing most of their "looking" online, it will not take up your time with those wasteful phone calls.) Clearly, then, a professionally-designed website could be an effective client-gathering tool. If you are interested in developing a professionally designed website please contact:

MentalHealthMarketingAcademy.com

Recently I saw the website of a licensed counselor that was quite well done. One thing which impressed me was that all the registration materials were available on the site and the client was encouraged to complete the forms and return them before their first appointment. (Wouldn't that be nice if you could have all the patient information ahead of time so you could verify the insurance at your leisure, assuming insurance was being used; but most importantly, you did not have to take so much time out of that first session with paperwork.) What especially intrigued me was that the site allowed new and continuing clients to book themselves into the available schedule.

Start a blog

As part of your website, you can and should start a blog. Blogging provides the opportunity to express yourself and to receive feedback. Blogging is another way to bring people to your website. Some blogs have become well known which can lead to the development of a "tribe"—a group of individuals who are involved with a particular concept or topic.

Podcasts

Just as with print media, more and more people today are customizing their audio inputs as well. People listen to their own choice of music, listen to audio books, and hear lectures on their iPods or EP3 players. Therefore, it makes great sense to attach audio files to your website that viewers can download. (You could also charge for the download, if you thought that was advisable.)

As I am writing this chapter, I am about to conduct a parenting seminar at a charter school. I will audio- or possibly videotape the seminar and attach it to my website. The more value you add to your site the more likely people will be able to find it and want to come to it—and, of course, ultimately want to see you and pay you.

By the way, if you have written any articles—or that book!—that material should be attached to your website as well so it can also be downloaded. A fee certainly could be charged to download the book. Wouldn't it be great if large numbers of people were regularly giving you their credit card number to download your book? What a great example of "passive income."

Other digital marketing

Mental health professionals should enter the digital age by employing the social networking sites of Facebook, MySpace, Linked-In, and Twitter. Enrolling in these sites is free though it will take some time to regularly update and work your site. These sites also have provisions for professional and commercial entities.

Frankly, early on I was not sold on the marketing value of these social networking sites until an incident occurred in my family which changed my mind. In September 2009 my son had a serious mountain-biking accident which led to a hospitalization. My wife and I had to leave at a moment's notice to care for and support him. When my wife and I returned home we had numerous e-mails and voice messages from friends and family all over the country inquiring about our son's status. When I asked how all these people learned about the incident before we contacted anyone, they all said that got their information from Face Book. I was truly impressed with how quickly the information spread. Thankfully, my son has recovered fully. Though this experience certainly scared us, as a secondary effect, I came to appreciate the value of these social networking sites as a potential marketing tool.

GOOD LUCK and GOOD MARKETING!

Important points to remember in CHATER TEN:

1. For mental health providers to flourish today, they must market their services and bring their marketing efforts into the digital age. Methods of doing such include: Begin an online electronic newsletter; develop a website using SEO; start a blog; attach a podcast to your website; and enroll in social networking sites.

Action steps to take from CHAPTER TEN:

1. Start gathering e-mail addresses of clients and referral sources and electronically send a monthly e-mailed newsletter.
2. Develop a professionally-designed website.
3. Start a blog.
4. Attach a podcast to your site.
5. Join a social networking site.
6. Make it a lot easier on yourself and contact MentalHealthMarketingAcademy.com.

BIBLIOGRAPHY

In preparation for this book, these are the resources I consulted:

Ackley, D.C., *Breaking Free of Managed Care: A Step-By-Step Guide to Regaining Control of Your Practice.* The Guilford Press; New York, 1997.

Auerbach, J. E., *Personal and Executive Coaching: The Complete Guide for Mental Health Professionals.* Executive College Press; Pismo Beach, California, 2001.

Blanchard, K., Hutson, D., & Willis, E., *The One Minute Entrepreneur.* Doubleday; New York, 2008.

Caldwell, M., *The Tipping Point: How Little Things Can Make A Big Difference.* Little, Brown and Company; New York, 2002.

Caldwell, M., *Blink.* Little, Brown & Co.; New York, 2007.

Collins, J., *Good to Great: Why Some Companies Make the Leap…and Others Don't.* HarperCollins; New York, 2001.

Collins, J., & Porras, J. I., *Built to Last: Successful Habits of Visionary Companies.* HarperCollins; New York, 2002.

Eker, T. H., *Secrets of the Millionaire Mind: Mastering the Inner Game of Wealth.* HarperCollins; New York, 2009.

Godin, S., *Tribes: We Need You to Lead Us.* Penguin Group; New York, 2008

Hayden, C. J., *Get Clients Now*, 2nd ed. AMACON; New York, 2007.

Hunt, H. A., *Essentials of Private Practice: Streamlining Costs, Procedures, and Policies for Less Stress.* W.W. Norton & Company; New York, 2007.

Lieberman, J. D., & Sales, B. D., *Scientific Jury Selection.* American Psychological Association; Washington, DC, 2007

Schultz, M., & Doerr, J.E., *Professional Services Marketing: How the Best Firms Build Premier Brands, Thriving Lead Generation Engines, and Cultures of Business Development Success.* John Wiley & Sons, Inc.; Hoboken, New Jersey, 2009.

Scott, D. M., *The New Rules of Marketing & PR: How to use News Releases, Blogs, Podcasting, Viral Marketing & Online Media to Reach Buyers Directly*. John Wiley & Sons; New York, 2007.

About Larry Waldman

I have lived in the Valley of the Sun (Phoenix/Scottsdale, Arizona) for nearly 40 years with my wife, Nan. Nan recently retired after 30 years of teaching fourth grade in the public schools. Nan and I have two sons, Josh, an attorney in southern California, and Chad, who is completing his training in school psychology in Portland, Oregon.

I started my private practice in 1979 after working for seven years as a school psychologist for Scottsdale Public Schools. Over the next 31 years I developed my private practice into one of the most successful practices in the Valley. During that time I learned many lessons about successfully—and not so successfully—developing, managing, and marketing a mental health practice. Although I read whatever I could get my hands on and asked questions of experienced mental health professionals whenever I could, I essentially was and have been on the road to private mental health practice on my own. Thus, as I approach the "twilight of my career," I have decided that I want to share what I have learned over these 30-plus years about private practice with other mental health providers—those already experienced in private practice and, of course, those professionals just starting out.

In addition to my clinical practice I do forensic work, consult to Social Security and to a private school, teach for Northern Arizona University, sell my books, and speak professionally. I've written four books during my career: *Who's Raising Who?: A Parent's Guide to Effective Child Discipline*, published in 1987, is aimed at helping parents learn how to use behavior modification procedures to effectively manage their children's behavior. *Coping With Your Adolescent,* published in 1994, is designed to help parents appropriately cope and shape their adolescent's behavior. *How Come I Love Him But Can't Live With Him?: Making Your Marriage Better,* published in 2004, teaches couples, using a behavioral model, to better understand their relationship and to behave toward each other in a more mutually-rewarding fashion. Of course, *The Graduate Course You Never Had*, which you just completed, was published in 2010.

I speak professionally to the community, to educators, and to other mental health professionals. Topics I speak on include, but are not limited to, the following:

Parenting and managing children's behavior; dealing with teens, marriage, stress management, understanding and treating ADHD; dealing with the difficult child in the classroom, solution-focused treatment, and private practice management and marketing.

To purchase any of my books, arrange to have me speak, or wish to have me consult to your private practice, please contact me at LarryWaldmanPhD@cox.net, or call me at 602-996-8619.

Thank you for taking your time to read my work. I hope you found the information to be useful.

Larry F. Waldman, Ph.D., ABPP

Publisher's Note

To learn about other fine books published under the UCS PRESS imprint, please go to www.marjimbooks.com.

LaVergne, TN USA
26 February 2010

174349LV00004B/2/P

9 780943 247977